MW01030454

SHAPED BY THE CROSS

MEDITATIONS ON THE

SUFFERINGS OF JESUS

KEN GIRE

IVP Books

An imprint of InterVarsity Press
Downers Grove, Illinois

InterVarsity Press
P.O. Box 1400, Downers Grove, IL 60515-1426
World Wide Web: www.ivpress.com
E-mail: email@ivpress.com

InterVarsity Press® is the book-publishing division of InterVarsity Christian Fellowship/USA®, a
movement of students and faculty active on campus at hundreds of universities, colleges and schools
of nursing in the United States of America, and a member movement of the International Fellowship
of Evangelical Students. For information about local and regional activities, write Public Relations
Dept., InterVarsity Christian Fellowship/USA, 6400 Schroeder Rd., P.O. Box 7895, Madison, WI
53707-7895, or visit the IVCF website at <www.intervarsity.org>.

All Scripture quotations, unless otherwise indicated, are taken from the The Holy Bible, New
International Version®, NIV® Copyright © 1973, 1978, 1984, 2011 by Biblica, Inc.™ Used by
permission. All rights reserved worldwide.

While all stories in this book are true, some names and identifying information in this book have
been changed to protect the privacy of the individuals involved.

Design: Cindy Kiple

Cover images: green textured background: © hudiemm/iStockphoto
            Pietà by Michelangelo: ©Steven Wynn/iStockphoto

Every effort has been made to trace and contact copyright holders for additional images used in this
book. The author will be pleased to rectify any omissions in future editions if notified by copyright
holders.

ISBN 978-0-8308-3808-0

Printed in the United States of America ∞

Library of Congress Cataloging-in-Publication Data

Gire, Ken.
  Shaped by the cross: meditations on the sufferings of Jesus / Ken
Gire.
      p. cm.
  Includes bibliographical references.
  ISBN 978-0-8308-3808-0 (pbk.: alk. paper)
  1. Jesus Christ—Crucifixion—Meditations. 2. Michelangelo
Buonarroti, 1475-1564. Piet 3. Suffering—Religious
aspects—Christianity—Meditations. I. Title.
  BT453.G57 2011
  232.96'3—dc23

                                                          2011032881

| P | 18 | 17 | 16 | 15 | 14 | 13 | 12 | 11 | 10 | 9 | 8 | 7 | 6 | 5 | 4 | 3 |
| Y | 26 | 25 | 24 | 23 | 22 | 21 | 20 | 19 | 18 | 17 | 16 | 15 | 14 | 13 | 12 |

To Howard Baker,

*who, when I first met him in college,
motivated me to be like Christ,
and who, after thirty years of friendship,
motivates me still.*

CONTENTS

We are all the work of your hand.

ISAIAH 64:8

ACKNOWLEDGMENTS

I would like to acknowledge my indebtedness to photographer Robert Hupka, who, during the 1964 World's Fair in New York City, where Michelangelo's *Pietà* was on display, was commissioned to photograph the sculpture for the Pavilion's souvenir record. Once Hupka started snapping his camera, he couldn't stop. From the time the statue was uncrated in April of 1964, to the time the ship carrying the statue back to Italy vanished from his sight in November of 1965, he took thousands of pictures. The work became, in his own words, "a work of love." The pictures were taken on different days, from different angles, in different lighting. Some were taken in color. Others in black and white. Some with 35mm lenses. Others with 400mm.

Hupka collected 150 of these photographs in his book *Michelangelo: Pietà*, six of which I have included in the book you are now reading. Hupka's book has a paragraph-long introduction and a two-and-a-half-page conclusion. Between them are his photographs. They sit alone on the page, without comment. Nothing stands between you and the images. Each page is a photograph taken from a different angle, emphasizing a different theme, evoking a different thought, eliciting a different emotion.

By the last page, you are a different person. Hupka's book is *that* powerful. The power is not in its words but in its images. And maybe there is something in that, something beyond the subject matter of the book itself.

A parable, of sorts.

The message is subliminal, likely unintentional, and perhaps I am making more of it than I should. But perhaps not. Perhaps there is something in the making of his book that can mentor us in the making of a life.

PROLOGUE

The conception of this book was not a planned pregnancy.

It originated as an illustration from Michelangelo's *Pietà* that I had planned to use in my previous book, *The Weathering Grace of God*. The book, however, had other plans. Each time I put it in, the book pushed it out. The illustration didn't fit, and the book knew it long before I did. Finally I realized why. Its inclusion in the book created a mixed metaphor.

In *The Weathering Grace of God* I used illustrations from nature, particularly the illustration of how mountains are formed. The illustration of the *Pietà* was from an entirely different set of images. I contacted my editor and told her that I felt *The Weathering Grace of God* wanted to be a smaller book than my contract specified. Half as long, in fact. The only way I could see to resolve the dilemma between my responsibility to the work and my contractual responsibilities was to do a companion volume built around the image of the *Pietà*. My editor graciously consented, and that is how this book was conceived.

The goal of both books is to demonstrate how God uses the circumstances of our lives, however confusing, to conform us to the image of his Son. *The Weathering Grace of God* focuses on the catastrophic upheavals that forever alter the landscape of our lives and how, over time, God beautifies that landscape. *Shaped by the Cross* focuses more on the everyday circumstances of our lives that chip away at the sometimes stubborn stone of the self to conform us to the image of Christ.

When I started the research for this book, I read a lot about sculpting, from the types of stone that were used to the types of tools. I read a lot about Michelangelo himself, not only from his letters and his poetry but also from his contemporaries and present-day authorities. Through a lot of interlibrary loans I was able to study photographs of his work. One book of photographs stood out among all the others, which is the work I refer to on the acknowledgment page. My personal reflections on the photographs not only helped shape this project but also my thinking of what it means to be conformed to the image of Christ, both individually, as a person, and collectively, as the body of Christ.

I have not seen the *Pietà* in person, but as I was sharing this project with a friend, he told me that he had seen it at the 1964 World's Fair in New York, where it was on loan from the Vatican. He and his family had stood in line for their turn to see this great work of art, and when their turn came they were moved on a conveyor past the sculpture, which stood some distance away. Twenty-seven million other people saw the *Pietà* over the course of the year, but, like my friend, they saw it only at a distance, and then only briefly.

What I want to do in this book is to stop the conveyor and give you an opportunity to draw close enough so you can reflect on this magnificent work of art.

Upon reflecting on a marble torso of Apollo, Rainer Maria Rilke wrote a poem about the encounter. The pillage of the centuries had cost the sculpture its head, its legs, its arms, yet something of its essence remained that seemed to live, seemed to stare back at the poet, telling him, "You must change your life." That is the power of art. The power to speak to the soul. With stirrings too deep for words, the *Pietà* doesn't say, "You must change your life." It simply changes it.

It has changed my life in ways I am only beginning to understand. I hope in spending time with the *Pietà* that you will be moved by it as well. I hope you will be moved to reflection. Then to your knees. And from your knees, to tears. And from your tears, to a deeper love for the Savior.

1

THE MYSTERY OF
THE PIETÀ

The Lord speaks in diverse ways: his deeds are words, as in the creation account we read, "He spoke and so it came to be." He speaks in the splendors of the universe and through all within it. He teaches in human language, and especially in the words of his incarnate Word. . . . But in all these manners the Lord is communicating through the beautiful, the true, and the good. . . . Thus God addresses us constantly through a snowflake, a tulip, a Mozart concerto, the Pietà.

THOMAS DUBAY, *THE EVIDENTIAL POWER OF BEAUTY*

If God addresses us constantly through the stars (Psalm 19:1-2), perhaps it is not too far a leap that Thomas Dubay makes in saying that God addresses us constantly through a snowflake. And if he speaks to us through the flowers (Matthew 6:28-30), surely tulips should be included in that sermon, wouldn't you think? If God speaks through the midnight choir that announced the Savior's birth (Luke 2:13-14), could he not also speak through a Mozart concerto? And if he speaks to us through the sculpture of salt that was Lot's wife (Luke 17:32-33), could he not also speak to us through the Pietà?

Not in the same way, perhaps, but certainly in some way.

Charles Rich thought so.

Charles Rich, a deeply spiritual friend of Robert Hupka, who opened the photographer's eyes to many profound insights about the Pietà, said this about the sculpture:

> There is so much in the Pietà that if you lived a thousand years and wrote a thousand books you can never express it. In other words, there is a divine quality in it. It must have been inspired, because how could a boy, twenty-four years old, create a work like that? You can't imagine how. It was a special grace from God. It is true, he had to be an artist, but art alone could have not made the Pietà.

The twenty-four-year-old boy who created the Pietà was Michelangelo Buonarroti. The artist, who lived to be almost ninety, has had many biographies written about him. Among them, one stands out: *The Agony and the Ecstasy* by Irving

Stone. What sets this biography apart from the others is that the author took the biographical details of Michelangelo's life and, instead of turning them into a dissertation, turned them into a drama. Though meticulously researched, his story is, first and foremost, just that: a story. In telling it, Stone made the artist's life accessible to millions, not only through his book but also through the movie that was adapted from it.

For those who haven't read the book or seen the movie, Michelangelo Buonarroti was born March 6, 1475, in Tuscany, Italy, and became, along with Leonardo da Vinci, the creative force behind the Italian Renaissance. He was a painter, sculptor and architect. Most of us know that. What many don't know is that he also wrote poems:

My unassisted heart is barren clay,
That of its native self can nothing feed:
Of good and pious works thou art the seed,
That quickens only where thou sayest it may:
Unless thou show to us thine own true way
No man can find it: Father! Thou must lead.

(Translated into English by William Wordsworth)

As the poem indicates, Michelangelo was a devout man who depended on God not only for his eternal life but for his everyday life. A letter to his nephew Leonardo underscores this: "I work out of love for God and put all my hope in Him." His passion for God and his passion for art were inextricably woven into a seamless garment that was his life, so much so that you could not pull on the thread of one without tugging at the other.

Michelangelo was the quintessential Renaissance man, producing over his lifetime a body of work that was as diverse as it was distinguished. He wrote poetry, sonnets mostly, but also madrigals, which are short love poems that can be set to music. He was chief architect for the construction of St. Peter's Basilica in Rome. His more noted paintings include the ceiling of the Sistine Chapel and *The Last Judgment*, which stands behind the chapel's altar. Two of his more famous sculptures are *Moses* and *David*. His most monumental achievement, though, is the *Pietà*.

The *Pietà* was commissioned by a French cardinal. The contract, dated August 27, 1498, stated:

> Let it be known and manifest to the reader of this document, that the Right Reverend Cardinal of St-Denis has agreed with the Florentine master sculptor Michelangelo, that the said master should make a Pietà of marble at his own expense, that is to say a Virgin Mary clothed, with the dead Christ in her arms, as large as a well-made man, for the price of four hundred and fifty gold ducats in papal gold, within the space of one year from the date of the beginning of the work.

The contract was guaranteed by the banker who owned the sculpture of *Bacchus,* which the artist had recently finished. The guarantee read: "And I Jacobo Gallo promise to the Right Reverend Monsignor that the said Michelangelo will do the said work within one year and that it will be the most beautiful work in marble found in Rome today and which no master could surpass today."

A lot of pressure for a twenty-three-year-old. Not only was the work to be unsurpassed in its beauty, it was to be *unsurpassable.* As if the young artist needed any more pressure, this unsurpassable work was to be finished in the unachievable deadline of *one year.*

When Michelangelo put the finishing touches on the *Pietà,* he was twenty-four. His final touch was to chisel his name on the ribbon that sashed Mary's garment.

"Michael Angelus Bonarotus Florent Faciebat."

Translated, the Latin reads, "Michelangelo Buonarroti of Florence made this." It was the only sculpture he ever signed. For five centuries, with only a couple of temporary moves, the sculpture has adorned St. Peter's Basilica, where it has been seen and revered by millions.

For the sculpture, Michelangelo searched the quarries for just the right type of stone. The marble he picked came from the Apuan mountains above the city of Carrara from a quarry that is still in operation today. It is the same quarry that provided the marble for the Arch of Constantine and the Theater of Marcellus, among other works. The various marbles at Carrara are themselves works of art, aswirl with color, from dappled Appaloosa grays to intricate laceworks of green. The variety of color is due to the mineral composition. Blue marble, for example, is due to the presence of graphite. Red marble, to the presence of iron oxide. And green marble, to the presence of chlorite and epidote.

Michelangelo often spent months in Carrara, where, with paternal care, he selected the marble, oversaw its extraction and arranged its transportation. The marble in Michelangelo's day was extracted from the quarry by drilling holes into the rock, inserting wooden wedges into the hole, then soaking the wedges in water. As the wedges expanded, they sent fissures running down the rock, causing the marble to break free in one massive block. The block was secured by ropes and eased out of the quarry on rollers until it could be put onto a cart and taken to the nearest harbor where it could find safe passage over the Mediterranean Sea.

Once the stout cube of marble arrived in his studio, the young Michelangelo went to work. He labored over it for almost two years, sweating over it in the sweltering heat of summer and shivering over it in the biting cold of winter. He lost weight, he took sick, but he never stopped. He was a man on a mission. A mission of liberation. He believed his figures were trapped inside the marble, and that if he listened to the stone, he could chip away everything that wasn't part of the figure, and the figure would be liberated. "I saw the angel in the marble," he once explained, "and carved until I set him free."

Look at the photograph of the *Pietà* at the beginning of chapter two and you can still see something of the quarry from which it was hewn, something of the marks of Michelangelo's chisel that freed the angels trapped within the stone.

The figures Michelangelo liberated from that slab of Carrara marble are more than angelic. There is a "divine quality" to them. Charles Rich was right. It had to be inspired. The artist had to have been given a special grace, for art alone could not have produced this. From the smooth folds of Mary's garment to the ragged gouges in Jesus' skin, the sculpture is exquisite in every detail.

Standing back, we see that, structurally, the marble is shaped like a pyramid. Within the pyramid is a cross. Mary forms the vertical beam. Jesus, the horizontal. The sculpture combines various levels of juxtapositions. Mother and son. Life and death. Sorrow and serenity. The fully clothed mother and the barely clothed son. The hand that clutches him and the one that releases him.

In order for the body of Christ to fit harmoniously within the structure of the pyramid, Michelangelo adjusted the proportions of his figures. Mary's arms and legs, for example, are exaggerated, but the exaggeration is hidden by the folds of her garment, and the casual observer doesn't notice it. Should the two figures be stood upright and placed side by side, Jesus would stand five feet, eight inches tall, and Mary would tower over him at seven feet, one inch. On the other hand, her face, which is not in proportion to her body, *is* in proportion to Christ's face.

From its overall structure to its smallest detail, the *Pietà* is a work of unsurpassed beauty. Michelangelo sculpted four *Pietà*s over the course of his life. The first one, pictured in this book, is known as St. Peter's *Pietà*, and resides in Rome. The Florentine and Palestrina *Pietà*s are in Florence. The Rondanini *Pietà,* in Milan. Sadly, the latter three never approached the magnificence of the first.

Giorgio Vasari, a contemporary of Michelangelo, published a book in 1550 titled *Lives of the Artists*, in which he praised the first *Pietà:*

> It would be impossible for any craftsman or sculptor no matter how brilliant ever to surpass the grace or design of this work, or try to cut and polish the marble with the skill that Michelangelo displayed. For the *Pieta* was a revelation of all the potentialities and force of the art of sculpture. Among the many beautiful features (in-

cluding the inspired draperies) this is notably demonstrated by the body of Christ itself. It would be impossible to find a body showing greater mastery of art and possessing more beautiful members, or a nude with more detail in the muscles, veins, and nerves stretched over their framework of bones, or a more deathly corpse. The lovely expression of the head, the harmony in the joints and attachments of the arms, legs, and trunk, and the fine tracery of the veins are all so wonderful that it is hard to believe that the hand of the artist could have executed this inspired and admirable work so perfectly and in so short a time. It is certainly a miracle that a formless block of stone could ever have been reduced to a perfection that nature is scarcely able to create in the flesh.

Looking at the sculpture today, even a photograph of it, causes similar reactions. Page through the photographs in this book. What thoughts do they awake in you? What feelings do they evoke?

With an almost gravitational pull, the sculpture draws you to itself. Can you sense it? As you gaze at it from different angles, it no longer seems marble but flesh and blood. And it no longer seems the gaze of your eyes that is taking it all in, but the gaze of your soul.

With timid reverence you reach out to the Savior's arm that drapes from his side. Then, in a merciful gesture, as you might kiss your fingers and touch them to the scrape on a child's knee, you touch your fingers to the slit the Roman spear has made in his side. The coolness of his skin warms under your hand, and a strange sensation comes over you.

You feel as if you have touched the very heart of God.

Your hand recoils. As it does, your thoughts are gathered into the long, flowing garment that envelopes the lifeless body of the Lord Jesus. You move your hand over the folds that lead to a face fairer than the moon in all its fullness. But it is not the fairness of the face that strikes you. It is the fullness of its sorrow. Something of it weights the lids of Mary's eyes. A trace of it lingers on her lips. You see the sadness in this mother's face. And slowly, imperceptibly, it becomes your sadness. But sadness is not all there is to see in that face. There is peace. God only knows how it got there, but it is there. And slowly too, imperceptibly too, it becomes your peace. In a way that only great art can, the *Pietà* reaches out to us, drawing us near, as if it has something to say, something it *wants* to say, *needs* to say. To us. To you and to me. It seems something hushed and serious with the weight of eternity bearing down on it. A mystery of some sort. The mystery involves the angel inside the marble. Who knows how deep a mystery it is? Or how dark? Or what will happen to us if we hear it? Horrible things, maybe. Or wonderful things. Who knows? Who knows what may be asked of us? Or given to us, for that matter? The railing that separates us in many ways protects us. Do we stay at the railing, a safe distance away? Or dare we draw near?

A PRAYER

Thank you, Lord,

For the art in galleries and the sculptures in sanctuaries that reach out and touch us, that draw us near and speak to us.

Especially I thank you for the Pietà.

Thank you for the heart that loved the angels in the marble and for hands that worked so hard to set them free.

I pray you would draw me near to this great work of art, Lord, so I can sense what you are wanting to say through it, and what you are wanting to say through it to me.

Thank you for the day of my separation from the quarry.

Thank you for the holes and for those who drilled them.

Thank you for the wedges and for those who drove them.

Thank you for the ropes and for those who held them.

Thank you for the rollers and for those who moved them.

So many people played such important parts in bringing me to you.

Most of all, Lord, thank you for pointing your finger at the stone and saying,

"That one. I want that one."

In Jesus' name I pray,

Amen

❖ ❖ ❖

FOR REFLECTION
OR CONVERSATION

Reflect on a time when you felt God speak to you through something that crossed your path—"not in the same way, perhaps," as God spoke to people in the Bible, "but certainly in some way." What made you think it was God speaking to you? How did you react? How did you respond?

When have you felt, like Michelangelo, that your "unassisted heart is barren clay"? Why are "good and pious works" so hard to come by?

"I saw the angel in the marble . . . and carved until I set him free." Think back on a time when you saw untapped potential in something—or someone. What did it take to set that potential free?

Imagine God "seeing the angel" in you. What has God done in your life to "set you free" for "good and pious works"? What still needs to be done?

Page through this book and look at the various photographs of the *Pietà*. What do you notice in your reaction to these images? Which part of the sculpture is most prominent in your imagination? Why do you think that is?

What do you think you could learn from the *Pietà*? What do you hope for God to do in you as you read through this book?

2

THE IMAGE OF GOD

*Then God said, "Let us make mankind in our image, in
our likeness, so that they may rule over the fish in the
sea and the birds in the sky, over the livestock and all
the wild animals, and over all the creatures that move
along the ground."*

*So God created mankind in his own image,
    in the image of God he created them;
    male and female he created them.*

GENESIS 1:26-27

The mystery is ancient. Unearthing it is like working an archaeological dig, finding potsherds here and there, and piecing them together to gain understanding of the lost civilization that made them.

Our search for understanding the mystery of the *Pietà* begins with an image.

In the ancient Near East the extent of a king's rule was marked by the placement of his image throughout his kingdom. An example in the Scriptures is when Nebuchadnezzar had a ninety-foot, golden image of himself made and placed it in the plain of Dura in Babylon (Daniel 3). An example outside the Scriptures is when Rameses II had his image carved out of rock at the mouth of a river, just north of Beirut, that flowed into the Mediterranean Sea. The image announced to everyone who saw it who the ruler of that area was, how strong he was and how greatly to be feared.

The symbolism of the image goes back further than Nebuchadnezzar, further than Rameses. It goes all the way back to the dawn of creation.

When God created the man and the woman, they were the crowning achievement in a gallery that was already filled with magnificent works of art, from the pinwheeled wonder of the galaxies to the darting iridescence of the hummingbird (Psalm 8). Of all God's creation, man and woman were his masterpiece. They were also the only work he modeled after himself (Genesis 1:26-27).

When God placed the man and the woman in the middle of the garden of Eden, they stood as living statues, so to speak, announcing his reign over that territory. They ruled as regents, standing in the place of and serving in the spirit of God himself. Their rule, consequently, was not dictatorial but custodial, serving as caretakers of the work of his hands (Genesis 2:15; Psalm 8:6). The mandate they received from God was not merely to rule the earth but to multiply and fill the earth (Genesis 1:28). It was through the multiplication of these images of God that the borders of his kingdom were expanded.

When Adam and Eve fell from their pedestal of innocence, the image of God suffered permanent damage (Genesis 3). With each sin, the image became more defaced (Genesis 4:1-16, 23-24). After generations of such defacement, barely a vestige of the divine resemblance remained (Genesis 6:5).

With an artist's grief, God destroyed much of the work of his hands (Genesis 6:6-7). But not all of it. He started over with Noah, as pure an image as he could find (Genesis 6:8-9). Even so, the vandalism of sin continued. Foreseeing that it would, God took measures to protect his image. In the same way museums sometimes go to extreme measures to protect their priceless works of art, God went to extreme measures to protect his.

Whoever sheds human blood,
     by humans shall their blood be shed;
for in the image of God
     has God made mankind. (Genesis 9:6)

Although in some cases the penalty served as a deterrent, that was not the reason it was imposed. It was imposed because irreparable damage had been done to the only work of God's hands that bore his likeness. Even a word spoken in harshness against the likeness of God is viewed in the Scriptures as a most serious offense (Matthew 5:21-22; James 3:9-12). In spite of how severe a penalty this was, though, it didn't stop the rampage of sin, which ran riot through each generation, wreaking havoc on our humanity.

Could nothing be done to repair the damage? Was there no deliverer? Was there no one who could restore the image of God on earth? Was there no hope for us?

There was. It lay embedded in Eden. Hacking away at the thorns and thistles that have overgrown it, we find a fragment of hope protruding from the ground.

> I will put enmity
>> between you and the woman,
>> and between your offspring and hers;
> he will crush your head,
>> and you will strike his heel. (Genesis 3:15)

From the context we know that God is speaking to the serpent responsible for the deception that led to the catastrophic fall of his image. Still, the message is difficult to decipher. Like the shard of an ancient hieroglyphic text, it is only a fragment, and a cryptic one at that. It seems a promise of some sort, but how it is to be fulfilled, when and by whom, is a mystery. There would be a fight of some sort. And a victory, it appears. But there would be a casualty too. How fierce would the fighting be? How soon would the victory come? Who is the one to be struck? And how severe a strike would it be?

Throughout the strata of biblical history, key finds are made that shine light on the obscurity of that first fragment of revelation found in Eden. The promised seed would come through Abraham (Genesis 12:3). He would be a descendant of David, and his reign would have no end (2 Samuel 7:12-16). His kingdom would be characterized by wisdom, understanding and fairness (Isaiah 11:1-5). His rule would regain the Paradise that had been lost in the Fall (Isaiah 11:6-9). He would bring justice to the earth, but he would do it with meekness and tenderness (Isaiah 42:1-4). And he would be born in Bethlehem (Micah 5:2).

Hopeful finds, each of them. And when they are fitted together an image emerges of a deliverer, a coming king whose mere presence on the throne subdues the entire earth. Each fragment of revelation heightens the anticipation of his coming.

Until *this* fragment—the fragment found in Isaiah 52:13–53:7, 10-12:

> See, my servant will act wisely;
>> he will be raised and lifted up and highly exalted.
> Just as there were many who were appalled at him—
>> his appearance was so disfigured beyond that of any
>>> human being
>> and his form marred beyond human likeness—
> so he will sprinkle many nations,
>> and kings will shut their mouths because of him.
> For what they were not told, they will see,
>> and what they have not heard, they will understand.
>
> Who has believed our message
>> and to whom has the arm of the LORD been revealed?
> He grew up before him like a tender shoot,
>> and like a root out of dry ground.

He had no beauty or majesty to attract us to him,
  nothing in his appearance that we should desire him.
He was despised and rejected by mankind,
  a man of suffering, and familiar with pain.
Like one from whom people hide their faces
  he was despised, and we held him in low esteem.

Surely he took up our pain
  and bore our suffering,
yet we considered him punished by God,
  stricken by him, and afflicted.
But he was pierced for our transgressions,
  he was crushed for our iniquities;
the punishment that brought us peace was on him,
  and by his wounds we are healed.
We all, like sheep, have gone astray,
  each of us has turned to our own way;
and the LORD has laid on him
  the iniquity of us all.

He was oppressed and afflicted,
  yet he did not open his mouth;
he was led like a lamb to the slaughter,
  and as a sheep before its shearers is silent,
  so he did not open his mouth. . . .

Yet it was the LORD's will to crush him and cause him
    to suffer,
  and though the LORD makes his life an offering for sin,
he will see his offspring and prolong his days,
  and the will of the LORD will prosper in his hand.

After he has suffered,
> he will see the light of life and be satisfied;
by his knowledge my righteous servant will justify many,
> and he will bear their iniquities.
Therefore I will give him a portion among the great,
> and he will divide the spoils with the strong,
because he poured out his life unto death,
> and was numbered with the transgressors.
For he bore the sin of many,
> and made intercession for the transgressors.

Imagine hearing this for the first time, the way the Jews in Isaiah's day heard it. Who could the prophet possibly be referring to? Certainly not the coming king. Someone else certainly, but who? A slave or a servant of some sort, that much is clear. The message is obscure, but it seems God has ordained this servant to suffer and to die. As strange as it seems, this pleases him and great good comes from it.

Here is the victory of Genesis 3:15. Here also is the casualty. And here is why. In his book *The Cost of Discipleship*, Dietrich Bonhoeffer explains:

> Since fallen man cannot rediscover and assimilate the form of God, the only way is for God to take the form of man and come to him. The Son of God who dwelt in the form of God the Father, lays aside that form, and comes to man in the form of a slave. The change of form, which could not take place in man, now takes place in God.

God sends his Son—here lies the only remedy. It is not enough to give man a new philosophy or a better religion. A Man comes to men.

The image of God has entered our midst—but it is not the same image as Adam bore in the primal glory of paradise. Rather, it is the image of one who enters a world of sin and death, who takes upon himself all the sorrows of humanity, who meekly bears God's wrath and judgment against sinners, and obeys his will with unswerving devotion, the Man born to poverty, the friend of publicans and sinners, the Man of sorrows, rejected of man and forsaken of God.

Here is God made man. It is too wonderful to imagine. And at the same time too horrible.

It is too wonderful that God would enter our midst to live among us, as one of us.

It is too horrible that he who stooped to shoulder the sorrows of humanity would himself become a man of sorrows, rejected by man and forsaken by God.

This is the mystery of the *Pietà*. This is what it cost the Son of God to become one of us. And something of what it will cost us to become like him.

A PRAYER

Dear Lord,

Help me to do nothing from selfishness or empty conceit, but, with humility of mind, let me regard other people as more important than myself, not looking out merely for my own interests but also for the interests of others.

Help me to have the same attitude that was in Jesus Christ, who, although he existed in the form of God, did not regard equality with God a thing to be grasped, but emptied himself, taking the form of a bondservant, and being made in the likeness of humans. And being found in appearance as a man, he humbled himself by becoming obedient to the point of death.

Thank you for not leaving him on that cross, Lord. Thank you for not only raising him but exalting him, bestowing on him a name which is above every name, that at the name of Jesus every knee should bow, of those who are in heaven, and on earth, and under the earth, and that every tongue confess that Jesus Christ is Lord, to the glory of God the Father.

Until that day, O God, grant that my knee would bow to him, my mouth confess him, and my life be worthy of him.

It is in his precious name I pray,

Amen

FOR REFLECTION
AND CONVERSATION

How does the idea of the Garden of Eden as a "gallery" change your way of thinking about creation? About human beings?

"Their rule . . . was not dictatorial but custodial, serving as caretakers of the works of his hands." What do you think is our responsibility to the world around us? What's the difference between "ruling" the world as dictators and "serving" the world "in the spirit of God himself"?

The author refers to sin as "vandalism." What is offensive about vandalism? Who is hurt by it? How might thinking of sin as "vandalism" change our attitude toward our own sin and the sins committed against us?

The Scriptures paint a complex picture of the One who will deliver us from evil: a wise, gracious and powerful king, on the one hand; and on the other, a suffering servant. Which picture comes closest to your mental image of Jesus? Which better resembles the Jesus portrayed in the *Pietà*?

"It is not enough to give man a new philosophy or a better religion." Why are these not enough? Why did Jesus need to come and die?

"This is what it cost the Son of God to become one of us. And something of what it will cost us to become like him." Reflect on the cost to Jesus of coming to us and dwelling among us, of dying on our behalf. Given this cost, what scares you about becoming like Jesus? What about becoming like Jesus gives you the most hope?

3

THE IMAGE OF CHRIST

"Now what is sculpture?" demanded Bertoldo [speaking to Michelangelo] in a mentor's tone. "It is the art which, by removing all that is superfluous from the material under treatment, reduces it to that form designed in the artist's mind."

IRVING STONE, *THE AGONY AND THE ECSTASY*

The struggle to establish God's rule on earth is not so much a battle of words as it is a battle of images. From movies to magazines to MTV, images dominate our culture. Their presence is inescapable. So is their influence.

It is impossible not to notice them and, at some level, impossible not to be influenced by them. We call them screen idols or teen idols or supermodels. And for good reason. We may not worship them, but we want to be like them. We envy their fame, we covet their fortunes, and, let's be honest, who of us wouldn't want their fans?

Our culture is a confusion of images.

So is our church.

We're not sure what it means to be like Christ. We're not sure what it means to see with his eyes, to hear with his ears, to feel with his heart. I wonder myself sometimes. I wonder what it is like to will only one thing, not to have a distracted mind or a divided heart. To want only what the Father wants. To love only what the Father loves. To do only what I see the Father doing. To speak only what the Father has taught me. I wonder what it is like to empty myself the way Jesus did. To give myself the way he did. To sacrifice myself the way he did.

As I gaze at the *Pietà*, all the larger-than-life images that once captured my imagination look so small by comparison, and so trivial. Someone once said that we don't judge great art; great art judges us. With the *Pietà* it is different. Here, we are not so much judged as we are saved. Saved from the tyranny of images that have filled the pantheon of our imagination.

Until Christ returns to establish his kingdom on the earth, God is restoring his rule in this rebel world, a person at a time, a family at a time, a church at a time. For now, the rule of God rests on those who bear his image, those whose lives reflect his love, his wisdom, his understanding, his compassion, his forgiveness, his humility, his gentleness.

Of course, not all who bear Christ's name bear his image. There is a difference between being a Christian and being conformed to the image of Christ. Becoming a Christian happens when the stone, so to speak, is freed from the mountain. A number of things happen beforehand to prepare for that moment, such as the drilling of the holes and the hammering of the wedges, but eventually, one final fissure sets the stone free. It may be a shattering moment in which the final crack reverberates through the quarry. Or it may be a silent moment in which the final crack is so slight as to go unnoticed. Either way, there is a moment in time in which the stone is set free.

Free from the mountain, that is. But not free from itself.

Becoming conformed to the image of Christ is the process God uses to free the stone from the self. Paul describes the process in Romans 8:28-29:

> And we know that in all things God works for the good of those who love him, who have been called according to his purpose. For those God foreknew he also predestined to be conformed to the image of his Son, that he might be the firstborn among many brothers and sisters.

God is using the circumstances of our lives, *all* the circumstances of our lives, as tools. He goes about his work the same way Michelangelo went about his. Within the rough-hewn stone of the self is trapped the image of Christ. To release the image, he chips away everything that isn't Jesus.

Just as the essence of sculpture is the loss of the stone, the essence of being conformed to the image of Christ is the loss of the self. For it is in losing the self, as Jesus said, that we find our best self, our most beautiful self, our truest self, our most eternal self. The self that is most like him.

We are God's workmanship, Paul says (Ephesians 2:10). That is the serious work of heaven. Making us like Christ. And God, as an impassioned artist, won't rest until that work is everything he envisioned it to be (Philippians 1:6).

In his book *The Story of Michelangelo's Pietà*, Irving Stone dramatizes the way Michelangelo worked, which he discovered by studying his letters, his journals and the accounts of his contemporaries. Here he illustrates the passion with which the artist worked on the unshaped slab of Carrara marble that was to become the great work of his hands.

> He carved in a fury from first light to dark, then threw himself across his bed, without supper and fully clothed, like a dead man. He awoke around midnight, refreshed, his mind seething with sculptural ideas, craving to get at the marble.

If Michelangelo worked this passionately on the *Pietà*, how much more passionately must God be working on his art? We are the work of his hands, and he carves in fury from light to dark. His mind is seething with sculptural ideas of what we will become. He didn't feel that way about the ruddy walls of the Grand Canyon when he carved them, or about the white cliffs of Dover when he chiseled them. But he feels that way about us. He craves to get at us, the way Michelangelo craved to get at the marble.

Irving Stone continues his description of how Michelangelo worked.

> He got up, nibbled at a heel of bread, lit the brass lamp in which he burned the dregs of the olive oil, and tried to set it at an angle that would throw light on the area he was carving. The light was too diffused. It was not safe to use a chisel.
>
> He bought some heavy paper, made a hat with a peak, tied a wire around the outside and in the center fashioned a loop big enough to hold a candle. The light, as he held his face a few inches from the marble, was bright and steady.

If you are the slab of marble, the scrutiny is, at best, uncomfortable. At worst, it is unbearable. *What is he looking for, and why is it taking him so long to find it? Why does he just stand there, staring? Why doesn't he say something?*

Sculptor Lorenzo Dominguez offers an insight into the artist's way, which also, I think, offers an insight into God's way.

> The material does not easily surrender itself to the sculptor. It is necessary to conquer it every day until you understand it. Only then does the material reveal its secrets, its intimate voices, its mysteries. This is not a knowledge that comes from chemistry or geology. This is not enough. It is necessary to know the material through love, before you can master it, taking

advantage of all its aesthetic possibilities. Each stone has its own composition, its own hardness, its color, its veins, its spots, and all this requires the use of different tools.

God holds his face a few inches from the stone of the self, and in the bright and steady light of his love he inspects us, noting the composition, its hardness, its color, its veins, its spots, to know exactly which tool to use and precisely where to use it.

The way God works is similar to the way Michelangelo worked, as he used different tools to achieve different results. He used the hammer, which was his primary tool, along with a variety of pointed chisels that he used to shape the block. Some chisels had serrated edges. Others were flat. Each had its own role in shaping the marble, its own special use, however slight. He also had an assortment of rasps and abrasives.

The tools of a torturer. Or so it seems.

From the perspective of the onlooker, when the artist begins his work, every blow from the hammer seems a random act of violence, every bite of the chisel, a senseless act of vandalism.

From the perspective of the slab, the blows it receives are even more difficult to comprehend. Who can blame the marble for not being able to make sense of what is happening to it? Who can blame it for its questions and its reactions? The waste seems so senseless. What purpose did it serve? What good did it accomplish? And who is the strange being that wields such a cruel hammer in one hand and such a cold chisel in the other?

In an untitled poem Michelangelo explained the process:

With chiselled touch
The stone unhewn and cold
Becomes a living mould.
The more the marble wastes,
The more the statue grows.

It is a confusing time for the work in progress. It is neither stone nor art, at home neither in the quarry nor the gallery. But bit by bit the slab grows smaller, and day by day its shape changes. Until one day, a shaft of sun angles from an open shutter to reveal the nature of the shape that is emerging. The features are unmistakable. It is rough-hewn but rounded. A head of some sort, a human head it seems. Within that head are the etched beginnings of eyes. Below them and between them, a jagged escarpment that appears to be a nose. And an elongated protrusion that, by its placement, can only be a mouth.

Day by day the work continues. The more the marble wastes, the more the statue grows. The eyes are now distinct.

Later, they will be deepened. Later still, they will be polished until peace shines from within them. The mouth is mysterious now. Later, the curvature of kindness will shape its lips. The work is now more sculpture than it is slab. The stone sees that something eternal is emerging from its embedded resistance. More and more it yields to the beauty it is becoming.

To the beauty it is becoming.

We are the work of his hands, you and I. Which is to say, we are roughly quarried stone on our way to becoming the *magnum opus* of God, the "great work" of his life. The work he thinks of, dreams of. The work he frets over, obsesses over.

We are a masterpiece in the making. And not just *any* masterpiece. *His* masterpiece. More magnificent than the *Pietà*.

The circumstances of our life, which God uses to craft our character, are often jarring, sometimes difficult to understand and difficult to endure. "What is required of us," advised the poet Rilke in times like these, "is that we love the difficult and learn to deal with it. In the difficult are the friendly forces, the hands that work on us."

The hands that work on us are God's hands. And just as Jesus worked beside his Father in the creation of the world, so he lends his hands in the crafting of our character. Those hands are sometimes near, touching the contours of our soul. Other times they are far, searching for a different tool. All times, though, they are purposeful. Their purpose is to make us beautiful.

The beauty of Christ is what we are destined for. It is also more than we ever bargained for. As C. S. Lewis noted:

> That is why He warned people to "count the cost" before becoming Christians. "Make no mistake," He says, "if you let me, I will make you perfect. The moment you put yourself in My hands, that is what you are in for. Nothing less, or other, than that. You have free will, and if you choose, you can push Me away. But if you do not push Me away, understand that I am going to see this job through. Whatever suffering it may cost you in your earthly life, whatever inconceivable purification it may cost you after death, whatever it costs Me, I will never

rest, nor let you rest, until you are literally perfect—until my Father can say without reservation that He is well pleased with you, as He said He was well pleased with me. This I can do and will do. But I will not do anything less."

A PRAYER

Dear Lord,

Thank you for all I am predestined to become, and for your persistence in seeing that I become it.

Help me to understand that the more the marble wastes, the more the statue grows.

Help me to love the person I am becoming more than I long for the person I am losing.

It is a difficult process, Lord, this losing of the self, and sometimes I can't understand what you are doing in my life.

Help me to see that in the difficult, as Rilke said, are the friendly forces, the hands that work on us.

More than I fear the hammer that is wielded against me, help me to love the hand that holds the hammer and keeps it from crushing me.

More than I doubt the chisel that gouges me, help me to trust the hand that guides the chisel and uses it to shape me into the beautiful image of Christ.

In his name I pray,

Amen

FOR REFLECTION
AND CONVERSATION

"The struggle to establish God's rule on earth is not so much a battle of words as it is a battle of images." How might images establish God's rule in ways that words couldn't?

Think back to the author's discussion (in chapter two) of man and woman in the garden as "living statues, so to speak, announcing [God's] reign over that territory." What picture of God do the dominant images of men and women today present?

"There is a difference between being a Christian and being conformed to the image of Christ." How would you characterize the difference? What tension have you felt between "being a Christian" and "being conformed to the image of Christ"?

"Just as the essence of sculpture is the loss of the stone, the essence of being conformed to the image of Christ is the loss of the self." In what ways might spiritual formation feel like a loss? Like torture?

"The material does not easily surrender itself to the sculptor." Reflect on some of the ways you have resisted God the Sculptor. What are you tempted to hide from God? Withhold from God? What helps you to yield to God's chiseling work?

"The work in progress . . . is neither stone nor art, at home neither in the quarry nor the gallery." Think back on times in your formation when you've felt this sense of homelessness, of formlessness. During these times, what has sustained you in the formation process? What could God offer you during such times to make the pain of transformation easier to endure?

"We are a masterpiece in the making." How often do you feel like this? What helps to remind you of the truth in it?

4

THE WOUNDS OF CHRIST

One perhaps does not even have to be a Christian to know that suffering belongs to the very nature of this our world and will not pass away until this world passes away. And beyond this, we Christians know that in a hidden way it is connected with man's reaching for the forbidden fruit, but that God can transform even this burden of a fallen world into a blessing and fill it with meaning.

HELMUT THIELICKE

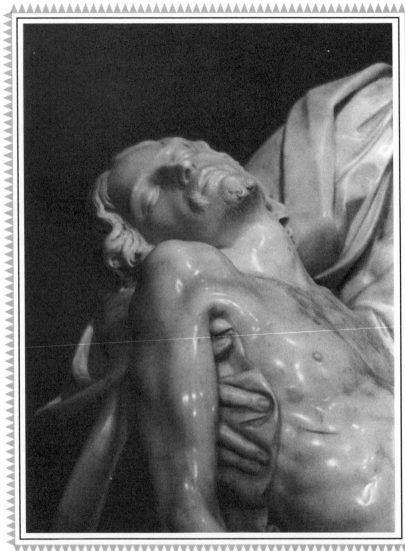

When I look at the *Pietà* from the angle in the photograph at the beginning of this chapter, the first thing I notice is the sheen on the marble, which in this lighting seems to be sweat on the Savior's skin. His flowing hair seems to disappear into the folds of Mary's garment. The weight of his head draws it back, pushing the neck forward, accentuating his Adam's apple.

Adam's apple. How ironic. How tragically ironic. Who would have thought, least of all Adam, that his choice would have led to this? Of all the fruit freely given in the garden, Adam reached for the one that was forbidden. And we have been reaching for it ever since. Which means that you and I have also had a hand in Christ's suffering. We share the responsibility for his wounds.

The slit in the Savior's side is where the upward angle of the spear had pierced his skin on its way to puncturing his heart. I see this, and I think of all the Roman hands that touched him, how many there were, how brutal they were.

I think of their hands, and it makes me think of all the other hands involved in Christ's death. I think of the Jewish hands that plotted against him, of the hands of the religious leaders who interrogated him. I think of the night of his suffering, and I realize that the first hand to strike Jesus was a religious hand. Another irony. The hands of the high priest turned him over to the hands of Herod, and his hands to the hands of Pilate, and his hands to the hands of soldiers, soldiers most likely conscripted from Syria, a country that hated the Jews. And Jesus being a Jew, the soldiers whipped him, mocked him and beat him mercilessly.

We follow a king whose victory came through defeat. The defeat came at the hands of his enemies.

He *was pierced* for our transgressions.

He *was crushed* for our iniquities.

He *was wounded* so we might be healed.

The verbs are passive. Other hands acted upon him. Different hands, all of them, but each an enemy. And prompting them all behind the scenes was the hand of his archenemy, Satan himself.

◆ ◆ ◆

At 11:30 a.m. on May 21, 1972, the day of Pentecost on the church's calendar, a crowd of worshipers was waiting inside St. Peter's Basilica to receive the blessing of the pope. Emerging from the crowd, a man darted past five uniformed guards, leaped over the railing in front of the *Pietà*, and pulling a hammer from his overcoat, he attacked the sculpture, shouting, "I am Jesus Christ! I am Jesus Christ!"

The madman who inflicted the damage was a thirty-three-year-old Australian geologist of Hungarian descent named Laszlo Toth. By the time he was subdued, he had hit the sculpture fifteen times, smashing Mary's face, knocking off her nose, chipping her eyelid and severing her left arm at the elbow.

For the restoration, the church assembled the world's best artists. When they arrived in Rome, they didn't begin work immediately. Day after day for weeks on end, they simply stood before this great work of art, looking at it, listening to it, straining to understand the artist's soul, what he saw in the marble, and what he was trying to say through it.

They ran their fingers over its smooth lines, touching

Mary's face, her elbow, touching also her wounds. They waited to start repairing the damage until they could see with Michelangelo's eyes. The work was slow and tedious, but finally, on March 25, 1973, it was finished, and the restored sculpture was unveiled to the public.

Before that crazed man took a hammer to the *Pietà*, precautions had been taken to protect it. It had been enshrined in a sacred place where the people who came were those most likely to respect it. A marble railing kept the crowds at a safe distance. Guards had been strategically placed to watch it. Yet that wasn't enough.

Will it be enough for us, I wonder?

The madman who leapt over the marble railing in St. Peter's Basilica and hammered Michelangelo's masterpiece is a vivid picture of Satan, showing us not only how destructive he is but how delusional. In jealous rage he seizes every opportunity to deface anything that bears a trace of divine beauty. Left unchecked, he will destroy it altogether.

But why does he take his hammer to *us?* Why not the trees or the animals? Are they not also the work of God's hands? Because we alone—not the trees or the animals—bear the image of God. And the more beautiful that image becomes, the more determined Satan becomes in destroying it.

Job, for instance. He was so beautiful a reflection of the image of God that God himself said, "There is no one on earth like him; he is blameless and upright, a man who fears God and shuns evil" (Job 1:8). Seeing him, Satan couldn't wait to jump over the railing that separated heaven and earth at the opportunity to take a hammer to him.

"Does Job fear God for nothing?" Satan replied. "Have

you not put a hedge around him and his household and everything he has? You have blessed the work of his hands, so that his flocks and herds are spread throughout the land. But now stretch out your hand and strike everything he has, and he will surely curse you to your face." (Job 1:9-11)

It seems, from the phrasing of Satan's request, that some kind of rules of engagement were being invoked, some form of military protocol, something determined between the two of them before the dawn of time.

Permission was granted, and parameters were established. "The LORD said to Satan, 'Very well, then, everything he has is in your power, but on the man himself do not lay a finger'" (Job 1:12). With repeated blows of his hammer, Satan wielded the fierceness of nearby enemies and the forces of nature against everyone and everything within those parameters.

Job's response to the randomness and senselessness of the brutality?

Naked I came from my mother's womb,
    and naked I will depart.
The LORD gave and the LORD has taken away;
    may the name of the LORD be praised. (Job 1:21)

Instead of falling on his sword, Job fell to his knees. Instead of raising a fist against his enemies, he raised a prayer. Instead of cursing the capricious hand of an onerous fate, he blessed the sovereign hand of a generous God.

Job's response enraged Satan all the more. So much so, that he asked for another shot at Job, this time to inflict bodily harm (Job 2:4-5).

Permission was granted, and the parameters were moved. "The LORD said to Satan, 'Very well, then, he is in your hands; but you must spare his life'" (Job 2:6).

The reasons for these rules of engagement have been kept from us, as well as what other rules may exist in the battle for the human heart. We are told in the Scriptures that a sovereign God rules the universe. We are also told that he grants permission that gives other forces their day of triumph within that universe.

The way he did with the Sabeans and Chaldeans who plundered Job's property (Job 1:13-17).

The way he did with the servant girl who questioned Peter's identity (Luke 22:54-62).

When Peter was most confused and most emotionally distraught, Satan "demanded" permission to get his hands on him (Luke 22:31-32 NASB). The request was voiced with greater intensity than with Job, for the battle being fought here was not simply for a human heart but for the human race. I'm paraphrasing now, but this is the gist of what Jesus conveyed to Peter. "Satan has demanded permission to hammer you like rock, but I have prayed for you that your faith may not be shattered." Satan's request was granted, but so was the Savior's. Peter emerged from the encounter severely chipped but not shattered.

The parameters that protected Job's life were fixed to limit the damage Satan could do. Then those parameters were moved, again by permission. Though suffering greatly, Job survived the ordeal and, by the gracious hand of God, later thrived (Job 42:10-17).

The parameters that protected Peter were fixed too, and

they remained fixed. He would fall into the hands of Satan, and though hammered by those hands, he would survive with his faith intact (Luke 22:31-32), later be restored (John 21:15-17), and would, as Jesus instructed him, return to strengthen his brothers (Acts).

The parameters that protected God's own Son, however, were not merely moved, they were lifted altogether. Again, by permission. "Don't you realize I have power either to free you or to crucify you?" Pilate asked Jesus during his interrogation. To which Jesus replied, "You would have no power over me if it were not given to you from above" (John 19:10-11).

The damage done by Satan's hands was devastating. We are told, prophetically, that Christ's appearance was marred more than any man (Isaiah 52:14), like one from whom men hide their face (Isaiah 53:3). He was pierced, crushed and scourged (Isaiah 53:5). He was oppressed and afflicted (Isaiah 53:7). Finally he was killed (Isaiah 53:8-9). A day of triumph for the enemy. Or so it seemed. It must have seemed that way too when the enemy had a similar day of triumph in China during the Boxer Rebellion. In an attempt to rid their country of the blight of foreign influence, Chinese revolutionaries went on a rampage and brutally murdered as many Christian missionaries as they could find. One such missionary, Edith Dobson, wrote in a letter dated April 26, 1900: "We are in the Lord's hands, and well we know naught can come to us without His permission, so we have no need to be troubled: it is not in my nature to fear physical harm, but I trust, if it came, His grace will be all-sufficient."

Shortly after that she was murdered. In the book *The Sister*

Martyrs of Ku Cheng, D. M. Berry questions the ways of God in the death of two particular missionaries:

> Why was it permitted? Why were lives so valuable cut off in the midst of work so important? A few minutes' warning (which numbers of friends not far off would have flown to give) would have sufficed to enable them to escape into the surrounding jungle. A friendly shower of rain might have been enough to turn back Chinese marauders from their purpose. But it was not to be.
>
> This terrible thing was permitted by Him without Whom not even a sparrow falls to the ground. He had spared and preserved them many times, but He did not spare them now.

He had spared and preserved them many times. But he did not spare them now. With Mr. Berry, I don't understand why. I don't understand why God would grant Satan's request, especially a request that would inflict such suffering on some of his most beloved children.

Yet he did. He did with them. He did with his own most beloved child. And though he has spared us and preserved us many times, one sad day he will not. Not even a sparrow falls to the ground apart from God's will, we are told. Yet every day a sparrow falls. And one day all of them will.

◆ ◆ ◆

In the lobby of Penrose-St. Francis Hospital in Colorado Springs is a small replica of the *Pietà*, encased in Plexiglas. The patients suffering at the hospital have been put there by the hands of their enemies. Cancer. Heart disease. Emphysema. Hepatitis. Pneumonia. The hands that struck them down are all different, but each is an enemy.

"He draws near to the brokenhearted," the Scriptures say, speaking of Christ, and when I realize that, I know why the *Pietà* has been placed there, for the Savior draws nearest to us in our suffering, and in our suffering we draw nearest to him.

It is startling when you think about it. "Every time we look at the *Pietà*," wrote Charles Rich,

> the startling quality of the figure of Christ becomes more startling. As we look at it with devotion and love, the soul is made to feel that this is the Christ, the God Who became Man out of love for the human race. All the sorrows we can experience in this life are assuaged by looking at the *Pietà*.

The *Pietà*, as resplendent as it is, is only a rough-cut rendering of the God who came to us, as one of us, to die for us. Yet even looking at a mere rendering of his love lightens the load of our sorrows.

And our questions.

Before that moment in his mother's arms, at a moment when he felt most forsaken, Jesus gathered what strength was left in him and cried out to the darkness that had overcome him. What he cried out was a question. That in itself should give dignity to *our* questions. However inadequately we word them, however intensely we express them, our questions have a place in our relationship with God. It is a sacred place. It is also a necessary place. We have to pass through it, completely and honestly, if we are ever to get to that most sacred of places, that place where we can say with

Jesus: "Father, into your hands I commit my spirit."

Trusting himself to the hands of his Father meant that Jesus would fall into other hands along the way. Hands of a betrayer. Hands of a prosecutor. Hands of an executioner.

Hands that would grab him, push him, strip him, beat him. Hands that would put thorns on him, impale him.

Trusting ourselves to the Father's hands doesn't mean we will not fall into other hands along the way. It doesn't mean we will be embraced by those other hands or even protected from them. It doesn't mean we will survive them, let alone triumph over them.

What it means is that behind all of those hands are his hands. It will be his hands that will one day bring those other hands to justice. That is what Jesus believed. And that is what gave him the strength, while being reviled on the cross, not to revile in return (1 Peter 2:23).

◆ ◆ ◆

When the German theologian Helmut Thielicke visited America in 1963, he traveled across the country, preaching every day and holding meetings where he discussed important questions with ministers, faculty members, college students and reporters. In one such discussion with students and journalists, someone asked him what he felt was the most important question of our time. It was the early 1960s, so you might guess the answer would be the race question or the nuclear question or the communist question. It was none of these. It was the question of how Americans deal with suffering.

The question of suffering, it seems to me, appears in the lexicon of Americans only at the place where things which are to be overcome are discussed. . . . All this leads to a wrong attitude toward suffering. Again and again I have the feeling that suffering is regarded as something which is fundamentally inadmissible, distressing, embarrassing, and not to be endured. Naturally we are called upon to combat and diminish suffering. All medical and social action is motivated by the perfectly justified passion for this goal. But the idea that suffering is a burden which can or even should be fundamentally and radically exterminated can only lead to disastrous illusions. . . .

We ought to become aware of how devastating can be the illusion that we can banish suffering from the world and that its extermination is the only task it presents to us. We must try to learn again that suffering must also be accepted, that it is sent to us and laid upon us, and that thus is one of the "pounds" with which we must "trade" (Luke 19:13). We Christians know from the gospel to what extent suffering is a raw material from which God wants to make something.

Our suffering, regardless of whose hands have inflicted it, is the raw material from which God wants to make something. Not even Satan's hands are powerful enough to keep *his* hands from transforming us.

Only *our* hands hold such power.

And perhaps that is the greater mystery, not why God permits other hands to touch us but why he permits *our* hands to prevent *his* hands from transforming our suffering into a blessing and filling it with meaning.

A PRAYER

Dear Man of Sorrows, so acquainted with grief,

Help me not to recoil from your wounds, not to fear touching them or to be touched by them.

Help me to understand that in my suffering I am not only nearest to you, but nearest to becoming like you.

It's a sobering thought, and I shudder when I think of it. Help me to understand that many of the sorrows I experience in this life belong to the nature of the world I live in, as the theologian said at the beginning of this chapter, and will not pass away until this world passes away. Thank you for being in the midst of those sorrows, transforming them into blessings and filling them with meaning.

For other sorrows that seem not of this world, senseless suffering that seems not from the hand of a heavenly Father, but from a hostile hand bent on destroying me, I ask that you would pray for me, Lord Jesus, as you did for Peter. Keep the hands you have allowed to strike me from shattering me, and use them instead in shaping me.

Amen

FOR REFLECTION
AND CONVERSATION

"You and I have also had a hand in Christ's suffering." Is that fair? Do you find it easy or hard to accept some responsibility for Christ's suffering? Why?

"In jealous rage [Satan] seizes every opportunity to deface anything that bears a trace of divine beauty." Describe your mental image of Satan. How does it compare to this image?

When have you concluded (or what would cause you to conclude) that you were being threatened or attacked by Satan? What did (or what would) you do about it?

Why would God indulge Satan's "request" or "demand" to cause harm to a person God created and loved? What can we do to recover from these times of trial?

"We Christians know from the gospel to what extent suffering is a raw material from which God wants to make something." What has God "made" of Christ's suffering? What has God made of sufferings you've gone through? What can you imagine God making of suffering you're experiencing now (or suffering you're observing in loved ones)?

In the midst of Jesus' suffering, the author suggests, he took comfort from his mother. What comfort can we offer to those around us who suffer?

5

THE MOTHER OF CHRIST

The power of one fair face makes my love sublime, for it has weaned my heart from low desires.

MICHELANGELO, FROM AN UNTITLED SONNET

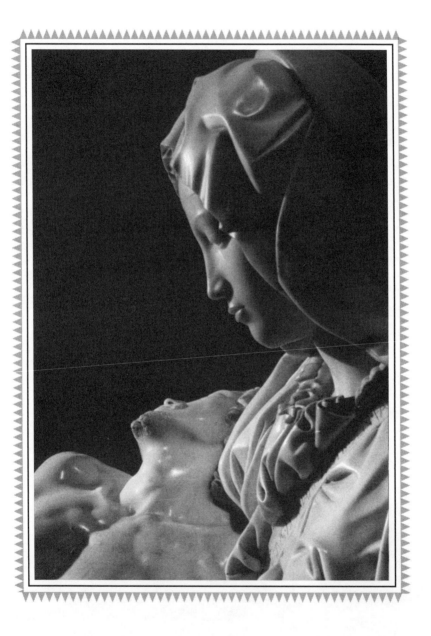

Mary, the mother of Jesus, was indeed most blessed of all women. Never has a human being been so intimately acquainted with God. God the Father chose her to be the mother of his only Son. God the Holy Spirit impregnated her. And God the Son lived within her.

Mary was chosen over all the women in the world to cradle the hope of the world in her arms. She nursed the Son of God, bathed him, clothed him. She walked with him, talked with him, played with him. She sang to him, told stories to him, tucked him into bed. Most of all, she loved him and was loved *by* him.

Hannah, mother of the prophet Samuel, was not so blessed.
Sarah, mother of the nation of Israel, was not so blessed.
Even Eve, mother of all the living, was not so blessed.
Mary alone holds this position of honor.

How many times when Jesus was a nursing baby had she held his squirming body in her arms, his naked flesh so warm against her breast?

Now this sudden stillness, this spreading coolness.

Her son has been cleaned up and covered up. He would have been naked on the cross, and the wounds in his hands and feet, those on his head, the one on his side, would all be mottled with blood. Some were fresh and red. Others, like the puncture wounds on his scalp, were hours old and mostly dried.

Who were the ones that cleaned him, I wonder? Joseph of Arimathea had left to ask Pilate for the body. Nicodemus had gone to gather the cloths and spices for his burial. Surely someone would have stepped in to keep his mother from doing such work. John would have certainly stopped her. Maybe it was the other women who were there that washed the blood from his wounds, the sweat from his skin, the spittle from his face and the handfuls of dirt that had been thrown at him.

Look at the earlier, full-length view of the sculpture. Washed from its wounds, the weight of Jesus' flesh sags at his torso. He seems to be falling, but somehow the strength of Mary's hand and the support of her legs steady him. The weight she bears on her lap is nothing compared to the one she bears in her heart. How heavy it must be. How wounded she must feel.

Who knows how deeply the presaged sword has pierced her heart?

Or how long her pain would last?

But her hands do not cover her heart, however wounded it is. One clutches her son. And the other? What is the other hand doing, suspended like that in the air? It seems a gesture of some sort. Is it a question her hand poses? If so, what could that question be?

And if not a question, what *does* the gesture mean?

Perhaps the answer is in Mary's face. Look at the photograph that begins this chapter. How tired her eyes seem. How heavy the lids. How downcast the gaze. Rilke's poem titled *Pietà* contains a fleeting reflection that Mary has when she looks down at her son, lying across her lap: "Now is my misery full, and namelessly it fills me."

Something of that misery is on her lips, in her eyes, in the tilt of her head.

Yet misery is not all that fills her.

The word *pietà* is Italian, meaning pity or sorrow. Over the years, however, it has come to mean the surrender of the soul to the sovereign will of God. Look again at Mary's face. Sorrow is there, that's true. But serenity is also there. It veils her sorrow, sheerly but unmistakably.

Thumb back to the full-length photo and study it. Her lap, it seems an altar, doesn't it? And her son, the sacrificial lamb. Her head is bowed over both. And her hand? Her hand seems a gestured prayer.

Henri Nouwen once wrote, "To pray means to open your hands before God." I believe Mary's hand is doing just that. In opening her hand to God, she is opening *herself*, surrendering herself, submitting herself to the sovereign will of God, however difficult it was to understand, however painful it was to endure.

◆ ◆ ◆

Losing a child is a parent's greatest fear. Mary lived with that fear all her life, ever since she brought Jesus to Jerusalem, where she heard Simeon's foreboding prophecy.

> This child is destined to cause the falling and rising of many in Israel, and to be a sign that will be spoken against, so that the thoughts of many hearts will be revealed. And a sword will pierce your own soul too. (Luke 2:34-35)

Every parent fears that a similar sword may await them. Every high temperature, every trauma, every trip to the hospital taps into that fear. One day with one of our children we experienced all three.

I was out of the office when it happened. Returning, I took

the elevator, and as soon as I reached my floor, our secretary, who had seen me drive into the parking lot, was standing in front of the elevator, waiting. When the doors opened, I saw her face, and instantly I knew something was wrong.

"You need to go straight to the hospital," she said, telling me that one of my daughters had had a seizure.

"How bad was it?"

"She stopped breathing."

I prayed all the way to the hospital. "Please don't let her die, God. Please. She's so young. She hasn't even had a chance at life. Please, Lord. Let her live. Let her live."

Our daughter had had seizures before, particularly when she got ear infections. Her temperature would shoot up from normal to 105 in a matter of minutes, and whenever it did, her body went into convulsions. They subsided after a few minutes, but those few minutes were terrifying because there was nothing we could do about it, except to try to keep her from biting her tongue.

When I arrived at the hospital, she'd already had blood drawn and tests done. She was sitting in a plastic tub half-full of water with a 105-degree temperature. As the doctors were determining the test results, my wife and I sponged her down. She was naked and shivering, and we could see the confusion through the tears in her eyes. She wanted her blanket, but all we could do was to give her the corner of it, which she brought to her mouth to suck. She couldn't under-stand why she hurt, why she was so hot and so cold at the same time. She couldn't understand why we wouldn't clothe her, hold her, rock her in our arms as we had done so many times before when she had cried.

Our hearts broke as we watched her shivering in that tub, her arms outstretched to us as we continued to pour more water on her. Though she was oblivious to it, we were suffering with her, and, at some level, suffering more.

How painful it must have been for the Father to see his Son on that cross, naked and shivering, not being able to hold him or put a blanket around him. Seeing him there, enflamed with such fever, all the while, the Son not understanding why his Father was so distant. Feeling so forsaken. Crying out, but not hearing his voice or experiencing his embrace.

I can't imagine the Father seeing all the shame and suffering his Son was going through and engaging in a theological discourse with the angels, explaining it to them with a steady and uninflected voice. I imagine, instead, a brooding silence so troubling to the angels as they saw it that none dared to speak, either to raise a question or to offer consolation. If there is such a thing as the tears of God, here must be where he wept them.

Regardless of whether you are a mother or a father, the desire to protect your children from pain is instinctive, especially from the pain of loss.

The children's writer Katherine Paterson wrote a book based on her son David's loss of a childhood friend. It was his best friend. Her name was Lisa. The book was *Bridge to Terabithia*, which won the Newbery Medal for the best children's book in the year it was published. In her acceptance speech, she described how Lisa's death affected her son:

> He is not fully healed. Perhaps he never will be, and I am beginning to believe that this is right. How many people in their whole lifetimes have a friend who is to them what

Lisa was to David? When you have such a gift, should you ever forget it? Of course he will forget a little. Even now he is making other friendships. His life will go on, though hers could not. And selfishly I want his pain to ease. But how can I say that I want him to "get over it," as though having loved and been loved were some sort of disease? I want the joy of knowing Lisa and the sorrow of losing her to be a part of him and to shape him into growing levels of caring and understanding, perhaps as an artist, but certainly as a person.

As a father who also wants his children's pain to ease, I want to shield them not only from death but from its shadow as it passes by. I want to shelter them from the sadness of friends who die young or family members who die old. I want to keep them from the frustration of flat tires and from the heartache of lost loves. I want to shelter them from the uncertainties of life as well as its tragedies. I want to keep them from scoliosis and emergency trips to the hospital, from high temperatures and febrile seizures.

I can't, of course. I know that. Still, I try.

How hard Mary must have prayed to spare her son from the pain he was suffering. How hard it must have been to watch as her prayers went unanswered. He was so close to her, yet so far from her. And that was hard too. She couldn't hold his hand, wipe his brow, touch a cup of water to his lips. His nakedness was exposed to all, but there was nothing she could do to cover him. There was nothing she could do to ease his pain. And that was part of *her* pain.

The heart that loves is a heart that has been made vulnerable by its loving. The more people we love, the more we will suffer. And the deeper our love, the deeper our suffering.

At some time or another I have suffered in some way with all my children. Suffered when one had been rejected by a classmate, when another had been rejected by a college. Suffered when one had a broken heart, when another had a broken arm. Suffered when they cried each time we moved, leaving old friends behind, and suffered as they struggled making new ones.

Like Katherine Paterson, I want their pain to ease. But also like her, I know that their joys and their sorrows will shape them into growing levels of understanding. Perhaps as artists, but certainly as human beings.

Michelangelo's insight into the heart of a parent was profound. Look at the fingers on Mary's hand and the way he has positioned them. One hand is holding on. The other has let go.

I try to hold on to them, to each of our four children who are now grown and out of the house. But I know I must let them go. In many ways I have. Still, it's not easy. And I'm not letting go of their life the way Mary had to. I'm merely letting them go to college, to marriage, to other cities, to other states.

They must live their lives, going wherever the hand of God leads them. They must experience their own joys, their own sorrows. Their own loves, their own losses. Still, I want to protect them from the pain that awaits them. Partly for their sakes. Partly also for mine, to protect me from the pain that their pain will inevitably bring to me.

Suffering is part of the process God uses in shaping us. I have come to the understanding that if I spare my children from the suffering, I will also be sparing them from the shaping. In doing so, I will be sparing them from the fellowship of Christ's suffering, from the deeper understanding that awaits them there, the deeper love that awaits them there, the deeper gratitude. And, as incongruous as it seems, the deeper joy.

This I have come to know is true. My children are not the work of my hands. My hands are not the hands that hold them, not the hands that mold them, not the hands that work all things together in their lives for good. They are the work of *God's* hands. I am merely a tool in those hands, a tool he has used in some way, for a short time, to shape them.

Tears fill my eyes as I write these words. I'm not sure why. Is it the "short time" that brings them? Or the "some way"? Maybe it's the "merely a tool." I don't know. This much I do know: though merely a tool, I am a tool that loves them. And though the tool may be used only in some way and only for a short time, it will love them in all ways and for all time. Even after the tool wears out and has been put away, the love it once had for them will live on in them. I hope so, anyway.

There has been joy in having my children at home, and sorrow in letting go of them. Those feelings, I have come to understand, are also tools, tools that God has used in some way, for a short time, in shaping me.

Perhaps as an artist.

But certainly as a human being.

A PRAYER

Thank you, Lord,

For the fair face that Michelangelo sculpted, and for the power of that face to elevate my love, and distance my heart from low desires.

In the sorrowful depths of Mary's loss, she somehow found the strength to surrender to your will, however difficult it was to understand, however painful it was to endure.

Grant me her strength, Lord, the strength to open my hands, not knowing what all you want me to give, knowing only that it is to your hands I give it. Help me to love those hands more than I love whatever it is I hold in mine. Help me to realize, Lord, that those I love are the work of your hands, not mine.

Yours are the hands that hold them, that mold them and that work all things together in their lives for good. Thank you for using me in their lives, in however small a way, for however short a time. And thank you, thank you so very much, for using them in mine.

Amen

FOR REFLECTION
AND CONVERSATION

"Her hands do not cover her heart, however wounded it is." Look at this chapter's image of the *Pietà* again. What do you think is communicated in how Mary holds her hands?

"Now is my misery full, and namelessly it fills me." Recall a time you felt despondent. How did your feelings shape your conduct? How you related to others? How you related to God?

"Her lap, it seems an altar, doesn't it? And her son, the sacrificial lamb." In what respect is being a Christian like being an altar? How does Christ's sacrifice on the cross relate to our day-to-day life?

"To pray means to open your hands before God." What does "surrendering to God" look like in day-to-day life?

"The more people we love, the more we will suffer." Why, then, do we love? What role does suffering play in loving?

The author reminds us that our children, and by extension all those we love, are not "the work of my hands. . . . They are the work of *God's* hands." How might this reminder shape how we love, care for, and support the people we love?

6

THE BODY OF CHRIST

A leper, speaking to a Jesus imprisoned in concrete: "What can be done to free you, Jesus, to make you live again so that you can come to us?"

Jesus: "My power alone is not enough. People like you must help to liberate me. Those who seek only the comforts, wealth, honor, and power of this world, who wish to carry the kingdom of heaven for themselves only and ignore the poor . . . cannot give me life again. . . . Only those, though very poor and suffering yourself, who are generous in spirit and seek to help the poor and the wretched can give me life again. You have helped give me life again. You removed the gold crown from my head and so freed my lips to speak. People like you will be my liberators."

THE GOLD-CROWNED JESUS

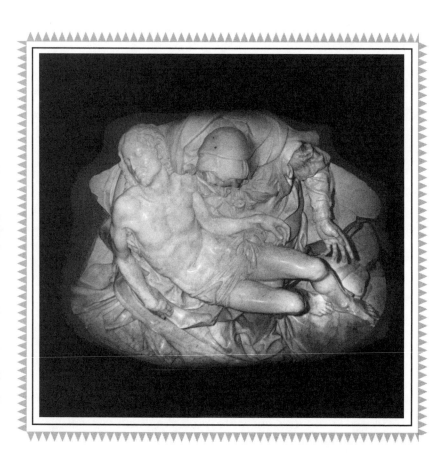

In the course of writing this book I traveled to Chicago with my son to see the Van Gogh exhibit on display at the Art Institute of Chicago. The weekend we were there we also visited the Field Museum of Natural History, which was displaying a rather prestigious exhibit of its own on Cleopatra.

The Cleopatra exhibit highlighted a variety of sculptures that gave context to her rule over Egypt and her alliance with Rome. Some were busts. Others, full-length statues. Some were intact. Others had noses, arms, portions of their heads broken off. Some had been carved out of marble. Others, out of basalt, limestone or granite.

The exhibition included Alexander the Great and the line of Ptolemaic rulers, with the succession of Cleopatras, of which there were seven. Cleopatra VII, who was the central figure of the exhibit, was the last and most famous in that line. Other world rulers were also on display: Julius Caesar, Octavian, Marcus Agrippa, Augustus and Mark Antony, Cleopatra's lover and political ally.

The diversity of rulers had been carved from different stone, but their features had been so idealized that it had blurred the distinctions between them. You saw the same qualities in Cleopatra, for example, that you did in Alexander the Great. The same regal posture, the same noble bone structure, the same strong set of the jaw, the same intelligent gaze.

Several full-length statues of Cleopatra were exhibited. Each stood erect with an ankh in one hand, the symbol of life, and a cornucopia in the other, the symbol of blessing. Her headdress was fronted with the puffed heads of three cobras, symbols of royalty.

The images stood in stark contrast to the image of the *Pietà*. Cleopatra in all her strength. Christ in all his weakness. Page back to the photograph at the beginning of this chapter. Of all the camera angles, this one captures the body of Christ in its most pathetic pose. Here Christ is held captive to the undignified pull of gravity, tugging at his arm, his legs, his torso. There is nothing noble about him, let alone, regal.

The body does not stand tall and erect. It lies across the lap of a woman, limp and lifeless. It isn't dressed in royal garb. A mere cloth covers him. His head has fallen to one side, exposing the neck. His eyes are shut. His muscles, slack. One arm falls from his torso. The other is wedged into his side. His legs are buckled at the knees and dangling.

If indeed this man was a king, it begs the question:

Of what kingdom?

Which begs another:

If we as representatives of that kingdom were made into a sculpture, what would it look like?

Would it look like Cleopatra, the ruler? Standing in control. The absolute power over life in one hand. The guarantee of blessings in the other.

Or would it look like Michelangelo's *David*, the warrior? Poised in strength. His slingshot in hand. His enemy in sight.

Or would it look like Michelangelo's *Moses*, the lawgiver? Seated in judgment. The tablets of the law in his hand. The sternness of the law on his face.

Or would it look like Jesus?

Not Jesus the teacher. Not Jesus the healer. Not Jesus the counselor. Not Jesus the prophet. Not Jesus the worker of signs and wonders.

Jesus the Savior.

The Jesus who emptied himself. The Jesus who gave up his place in heaven, who gave up the powers of deity and the privileges of royalty. The Jesus who gave up his reputation. The Jesus who gave up the seat of honor to become a servant. The Jesus who gave his love, his understanding, his compassion, his forgiveness. The Jesus who gave and gave and gave, until at last there was nothing left to give. Except his life. And then he gave that too.

Jesus died, Paul says, "that those who live should no longer live for themselves but for him who died for them and was raised again" (2 Corinthians 5:15). The cross creates a Copernican shift in the solar system that revolves around the self. The small spinning planet that is my life is not the center of that solar system as I once imagined and at times still imagine. Jesus is the center. The axis of that center is the cross. The entire universe orbits around it. When we align ourselves to that axis, we are no longer drawn to live for ourselves but for him. And in living for him, we begin putting others before ourselves the way he did (Philippians 2:3-5).

This is the image of Jesus in the *Pietà*. It is the image of someone dying to the self and all its hyphenates: self-interest, self-reliance, self-indulgence, self-protection, self-preservation, self-promotion.

Is that the image people see in us, I wonder? Is that the image they see in the pulpit, hear on the radio, view on the television?

I was watching television one Sunday, sitting on the couch and thumbing the remote as images shuffled across the screen. The image I stopped on was a bantam rooster of a man, strutting across the stage, so sure of himself and his formula for prosperity. Give a dollar, get ten in return. Give ten, get a hundred. Give a hundred, get a thousand.

The image repulsed me.

We give, not to get but because there is a need. Because it is the right thing to do. Because it is what Jesus would do if he were here. And that is precisely how he *is* here. Through us. He is born into this world again through every act of kindness we show to others. Through us his love is incarnate. Through us the invisible becomes visible, the Word becomes flesh, again.

Conversely, through us his image can also become distorted. Look at the images of him we have given the world. Images like Cleopatra that are so absolute in their claims to hold the power of health and wealth in their hands. Images like David that have their political muscles flexed, poised to boycott, votes in hand, ready to be cast against whatever cultural Goliath may be taunting us. Or images like Moses that are seated on their thrones of judgment with their stern faces and their Bibles breasted to them as rigidly as tablets of stone.

If those are the images we have given the world, can we blame the world for giving them back? They give them back in a number of different ways. Dismissive ways, mostly. And ways that are critical, sometimes even confrontative. Other times they give back the images to us on film. Sometimes the images are caricatures. Other times they are honest portrayals.

I am thinking out loud here, but could it possibly be that the images of Christians projected on movie screens are the same images we have projected to the world?

I'm thinking of Daryl Hannah's portrayal of a Christian in the movie *Steel Magnolias*. Her faith is simplistic. Her conversations, full of platitudes. And she is so out of touch with the people around her.

I'm thinking of the character Woody Allen plays in *Hannah and Her Sisters,* who tries Christianity but finds it full of crass commercialism and self-serving promises.

I'm thinking of *At Play in the Fields of the Lord*, which presents a cross-section of the church as a dysfunctional family with bitter competition between the Protestant and Catholic missionaries, vying over the territory of lost souls.

If we, as Christians, recoil from such images, imagine what it is like for those who aren't Christians to get stuck at a social gathering with a roomful of such images.

One of those images caused me not so much to recoil from it as to reflect on it. I saw the image in a scene from the movie *With Honors*. It was only on screen for a few seconds, but it has stayed with me a long time, along with the soft-spoken criticism it conveyed.

The movie is about a relationship that develops between a Harvard student, played by Brendan Fraser, and a homeless man, played by Joe Pesci. Fraser is trying to graduate with honors, and the only thing he needs to do this is finish his thesis. The thesis is titled "The Bottomless Well of Need" and examines the role of the government in helping the homeless.

The plot begins when Fraser's hard drive on his computer crashes, endangering his chances of completing the thesis on time. He takes the only copy he has of his thesis, puts it in a manila envelope and runs out of his dorm to get it photocopied. As he is running, he slips on the icy sidewalk. The envelope falls down a stairwell into an open window of the library's boiler room. By the time Fraser enters the room, he sees the homeless Pesci feeding his thesis to the incinerator, a page at a time.

Fraser is aghast. He tries reasoning with Pesci, but gets nowhere. Exasperated, he pleads.

"You don't understand. That's my life."

"What? Your life is a bunch of paper?" Pesci replies.

Seeing how much it means to the boy, Pesci offers him a deal. For each kind thing the boy does for him, Pesci agrees to give him a page. For each night's shelter, for example, Pesci gives him a page. For each meal, he gives him another page. For a hot bath, he gives him two pages. And so the story goes. The thin, white pages of the thesis become the sacrament through which their friendship develops.

In the course of their friendship, Fraser discovers that the man is dying. He seeks government help, but gets nowhere. Pesci is resigned to his fate and, wanting to die alone, disappears.

One day, Fraser hears a knock on the door. It is a homeless friend of Pesci's, who has come to return the remaining pages of the boy's thesis. Fraser asks where his friend is.

"If you ask, I'm not supposed to tell you, but it's St. Peter's Church Shelter."

That night, Fraser finds St. Peter's Church. The scene begins with the camera framing a tall cross carved out of stone with Jesus nailed to it. Behind him is a beautiful stained-glass window. The camera pans down slowly over the body of Christ to find the boy knocking at the massive oak doors. A man answers.

"Where's the men's shelter?" Fraser asks.

"Shelter? There's no shelter here," the man answers.

"You sure?"

"Worked here for thirty-two years. I ought to know. Closest thing we got to a shelter is over there in the alley." The man points to an alley that is littered with the homeless. Some are warming themselves around a fire. Others sit huddled against the cold. Still others are sleeping in cardboard boxes. As Fraser walks down the steps of the church, the camera pulls back to reveal the cross we saw at the beginning of the scene. We see the arms of Christ outstretched, as if reaching out to embrace those in the alley. At the same time, we see the Christian in the church close its massive doors and disappear inside.

Is this another example of Hollywood's longstanding grudge against Christianity? Or is it a plea? A plea to come out of our churches and into the alleyways of the brokenhearted. A plea to reach out to them, the way Fraser did. A plea to love them and to serve them. A plea to be what we are called to be.

The body of Christ.

Eugene Peterson's translation of John 1:14 in *The Message* hints at what it means to be the body of Christ in the world. It reads, "The Word became flesh and blood, and moved into the neighborhood."

As the body of Christ, we move into the neighborhoods of other people's lives. We move there to love them, to serve them, to give ourselves to them, and in doing so to show them Jesus.

As C. S. Lewis emphatically underscored in his book *Mere Christianity:*

This is the whole of Christianity. There is nothing else. It is easy to get muddled about that. It is easy to think that the Church has a lot of different objects—education, building, missions, holding services. . . . The Church exists for nothing else but to draw men into Christ, to make them little Christs. If they are not doing that, all the cathedrals, clergy, missions, sermons, even the Bible itself, are simply a waste of time. God became man for no other purpose.

The Bible reveals most of what we know about Jesus. Here and there, though, we get glimpses of him in other places, in the lives of those who live among us and of those who went before us. I'm thinking of Mother Teresa. She didn't begin her ministry with a mission statement or a donor base. There were no plans, no programs, no focus groups. There was just this wisp of a woman who saw an abandoned, sick child crying in the street, and her heart went out to it. She picked it up, held it, took care of it. That moment, in the manger of a woman's heart, a Savior was born. And the world that sat in darkness once again saw a great light.

Out of the darkness of September 11, 2001, the world saw another great light. Perhaps you saw it too in a photograph on the nightly news or in the morning paper.

In the photograph a group of firemen and emergency workers are carrying the dead body of a firehouse chaplain who died in the World Trade Center disaster. The slump of lifeless flesh they were carrying was Father Mychal Judge.

Father Mychal was chaplain to a group of firefighters in New York City. As soon as he heard a plane had slammed into the side of the World Trade Center, he rushed to the scene of the disaster with two of his firefighter friends. Once there, they went to work. The firefighters raced to the building. Father Mychal raced to the hurting. From the fiery inferno of the upper stories, a woman jumped to her death, hitting a fireman on the street below. Father Mychal ran to help them. The woman died instantly, and the fireman was on the verge of dying. The chaplain removed his helmet to administer last rites to the man, and, as he did, was hit by falling debris and killed.

Later that day several firemen and emergency workers pulled him from the rubble. They carried his ash-covered body to St. Peter's Catholic Church and laid him on the altar, covering him with a white sheet and placing his helmet on his chest.

Father Mychal lived among the firemen of New York City, not as a preacher or a program director. As a servant. He was there in the ups and downs of their everyday life. And he was there on this catastrophic day that cost so many of them their lives. Instead of standing a safe distance from the disaster or waiting back at the firehouse for them to return, Father Mychal went into the neighborhood of the disaster with them, as one of them.

Like anyone else, I am influenced by the images surrounding me, sometimes confused by those images. And like anyone else, I sometimes lose sight of what it means to be the body of Christ. Then I see the photograph of Father Mychal's limp and lifeless body. And suddenly everything is clear. I don't need a church council to determine it. I don't need a theologian to define it. I don't need a denomination to vote on it. I have all I need in that one image. When I look at it, the Spirit of God bears witness, and I know with great conviction that this is what it means for us to be the body of Christ.

When I look at that picture, I don't see a patriot, I don't see a Catholic, I don't even see a chaplain. I see Jesus. Those around him saw Jesus too.

The image of those men carrying Father Mychal's body is a modern-day *Pietà*. That they carried him to a church, that they placed him on an altar, that they covered him with a sheet, that they placed on him a helmet, all of these actions speak volumes about their love for him, their respect for him, their devotion to him who gave his last ounce of devotion for them.

When I think of what they did, it reminds me of what Nicodemus and Joseph of Arimathea did for Jesus, carrying his body to a nearby garden, wrapping it for burial, putting it on a stone slab in a new tomb and placing a cloth over his face.

Who knows the effect it had on them to carry away the body of Jesus? Who knows the effect it had on those firemen to carry away the body of Father Mychal?

None of them will ever forget it, I'm sure.

The terrorist attack on the World Trade Center was a disaster that affected the entire world. People expressed their grief for the victims and their devotion to them in a number of different ways. Some of them unfurled a rectangular white sheet from the top of a nearby building with the words in large black letters,

WE WILL NEVER FORGET.

The same words suddenly began appearing everywhere. On front pages of newspapers. On covers of magazines. On coverage from the Fox News Network, CNN and other stations. On poster boards. Billboards. Bumper stickers.

WE WILL NEVER FORGET.

"Do this in remembrance of me," Jesus said as he broke the bread and gave it to his disciples, saying, "This is my body given for you." In the same way, Jesus took the cup of wine and gave it to them, saying, "This cup is the new covenant in my blood, which is poured out for you" (Luke 22:19-20).

What is it that Jesus is wanting us to remember about him? The way he preached? The way he healed? The way he confronted hypocrisy? The way he fed the five thousand, calmed the sea, cast out demons?

No. Look at the context. *My body which is given for you. My blood which is poured out for you.* Jesus wants us to remember his death because his dying shows us so much about living. "We always carry around *in our body* the death of Jesus," Paul tells us, "so that the life of Jesus may also be revealed *in our body*" (2 Corinthians 4:10, emphasis added). The old self must die so that the new self may live.

The closer we are to the cross of Christ, the closer we are to our true humanity, the humanity that most reflects the image of Christ. There was no bickering at the foot of the cross. There was no one asking for lightning to fall in judgment on some unreceptive city. There was no one debating who the greatest in the kingdom was. There was no one quibbling over seating arrangements. There was no one weighing what he had given up and wondering what he would get back in return.

There was none of that. There was only the undying love of a dying Savior. Before Jesus went to his death, he stated his last will and testament. "As I have loved you, *so you must love one another*" (John 13:34, emphasis added). He showed us how he loved us on the cross. That is what we are to remember. And that is how we are to live. When we take the sacrament of Communion, Paul says, we proclaim the Lord's death until he comes (1 Corinthians 11:26).

We are, in essence, unfurling a banner that reads: "WE WILL NEVER FORGET." Our remembrance of the Savior's death is one of the tools God uses in shaping us. Of all the tools at his disposal, it is the sharpest, the steadiest and the surest. Perhaps it is also the gentlest.

A PRAYER

Dear Lord Jesus,

Help me to realize that I am part of a body of people that has been placed here to represent you. Help me to understand what it means to be the body of Christ and then to be it. Thank you for Mother Teresa of Calcutta and for Father Mychal of New York City, and for all those who in some way have shown me through their face, your face.

Who have shown me through their eyes, your eyes, through their hands, your hands, through their heart, your heart, and through their sacrifice, your sacrifice.

Bless them, Lord, for all they have done to help liberate you in my life.

Please know that all they have done for me will serve as a reminder of all you have done for me. I will never forget the body you gave for me or the blood you poured out for me. For something so beautiful to remember, I thank you, Lord Jesus. And I thank you for the deliverance that comes through this remembrance.

Amen

FOR REFLECTION
AND CONVERSATION

"If we as representatives of that kingdom were made into a sculpture, what would it look like?" What's your mental image of the typical Christian?

"Through us . . . the Word becomes flesh, again." How does this idea, that Christ is present to this world by means of us, influence the way you practice your faith?

How do you think Christians are typically portrayed in books, film and television? How do you think Christians typically portray themselves in the public eye? Which do you think is more accurate? Why?

"The Church exists for nothing else but to draw men into Christ, to make them little Christs. . . . God became man for no other purpose." What other purposes distract the church from this mission? What other purposes distract you from this mission?

"The closer we are to the cross of Christ, the closer we are to our true humanity." What can you do today to draw closer to the cross of Christ, and thus closer to your true humanity?

7

THE MIRACLE OF
THE RESURRECTION

"What an extraordinary place!" cried Lucy. "All those stone animals—and people too! It's—it's like a museum!"

"Hush," said Susan, "Aslan's doing something."

He was indeed. He had bound up to the stone lion and breathed on him. Then without waiting a moment he whisked round—almost as if he had been a cat chasing its tail—and breathed also on the stone dwarf, which (as you remember) was standing a few feet from the lion with his back to it. . . .

Everywhere the statues were coming to life. The courtyard no longer looked like a museum; it looked more like a zoo.

C. S. LEWIS, THE LION, THE WITCH, AND THE WARDROBE

❀ ❀ ❀

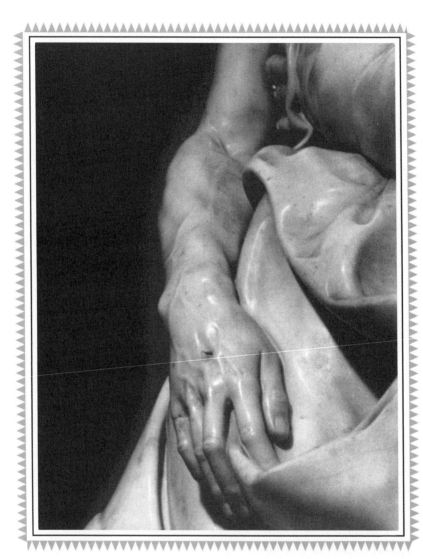

Sabbath descended on the holy city, slowly, somberly, as if a merciful curtain coming down on a tragic ending to the story you longed with all your heart to end any way but this way.

The light of the world had been extinguished.

And so had the hopes of those who loved him.

"We must make haste," Joseph said, looking at the descending sun.

Everyone went to work. Two men planted a ladder at the base of the center cross, resting it against the back of the crossbeam. Nicodemus steadied it as Joseph stepped onto the first rung. With each rung his legs grew heavier.

Once on top, he bent over the beam. The hole in Jesus' wrist was much larger than the nail, and he could see the bloody whiteness of his bones, the fraying pink of his muscles. He lifted an arm gingerly over the nail, and it fell, the weight of the body shifting to one side. He lifted the other arm and waited until those below were in position to catch him. As Joseph jostled the arm from the nail that held it, the body fell forward.

Nicodemus, John and a few other men caught him. His body was slick with blood. Holding him was slippery work, unsteady work, unbearable work.

One of the women eased his foot from the nail that impaled it, and he was free.

They laid him on the ground. Both shoulders were dislocated. On one, a flap of skin was folded to one side, exposing cartilage and ligaments at the end of a ragged weave of muscle. His face was swollen from Roman fists; his flesh, torn by

Roman whips. The contours of Jesus' body seemed a war-torn landscape in the aftermath of battle. The sunken muscles seemed like sloping hills, trodden under the enemy's brutal heel, the soil stained with the blood of fallen warriors.

A mist of unspoken questions rose from the landscape. *If there were such a place as Paradise, as this deposed king said, are the ragged borders of his body the terrain that led there; might the blood seeping from his wounds be the tributaries that led to its source?*

It was all so clear once, and so compelling. Now, it was incomprehensible. Totally and utterly incomprehensible.

But it was no time for introspection. It was time for action.

All of them wanted privacy to prepare the body for burial, and so several of his followers bent over it, grasped the arms, the legs, the torso, and lifted it in one movement. They carried it forty yards or so to a garden below the hill. The garden was enclosed by a wall of low stones. Inside, the shrubbery had been well tended. They put the body down and paused to catch their breaths.

They laid it in front of Joseph's tomb, recently hewn out of a wall of rock, cropping out from the hillside. Hardly a work of art. It was limestone, not marble. Who knows who did the work? It was not the work of an artist but rather that of a common laborer working with a mallet and a chisel. Chipping away mindlessly. Removing the splintered rock a bucket at a time. Day-in, day-out. An artless, joyless, monotonous job. Not the kind of work that anyone, when finished, was tempted to sign.

It was one among many tombs carved into the hillside.

Each one held a white statue of a once-vibrant story that now lay lifeless in a museum of slowly decaying memories.

The women came with a bucket of water and knelt beside the men. Taking out a Mediterranean sponge that was soaking inside it, Mary Magdalene began washing away the cruelty of Roman hands. Others took the corners of their garments and dipped them into the bucket, touching them to Jesus' skin, dabbing up the blood.

With his arm around Jesus' mother, John led her to her son. No one said anything. As she knelt, the others made room for her. She moved her hand over her son's chest, touching the wound in his side. She stroked the face, delicately, as a mother would stroke the face of her sleeping child. She cradled his head with her hand, pulling him to her. John and Mary helped lift the body. She folded herself over it, drawing its limpness into her chest. As she rocked him, she sobbed.

The others touched her arms, her shoulders, leaned their head against hers and wept. Slowly, then, she laid the body down. John offered his hand. She looked at it, blankly at first, looked at her son, then back at John. He wanted to be strong for her, to say something that might comfort her, but when he opened his mouth, no words came. His hand trembled. She took it in hers, placing her other hand on top of it, imparting a measure of strength. And with that strength, he pulled her to her feet.

The sun was losing its fullness on the horizon, the way of an egg as it fries. The body had to be in the tomb before the first star appeared in the sky.

No one spoke. They all knew the ritual. They wrapped the body in linen cloths, sprinkling between the layers spices that were pungent with yesterday's life, cool and dark and loamy. This is how it was done. A tight wrapping of linen. A sprinkling of spices. Then again. And again. Until the body was stiff and white as a statue.

After the process was complete, one by one they put a hand on the stiff linen—on its face, its shoulder, its chest, its legs, its feet. With those final touches, they said their good-byes. A sigh. A moan. A sudden spill of tears.

The sun had broken now, spilling its yoke over the landscape. Some of that light found its way into the garden. A breeze rustled through the leaves on the trees that spread low branches over the garden, as if servants fanning the small group of mourners.

They picked up the body and carried it to the front of a tomb, its whiteness in contrast to the weathered stone around it, giving evidence it had been recently hewn. A trough had been chiseled outside the tomb, where a millstone rested on its side so it could be rolled to close the entrance.

They placed the wrapped body on a stone slab inside the tomb, stayed there a moment, then withdrew. The men rolled the stone into place. As the sun slipped beneath the horizon, they left.

The fullness of the Passover moon ladled its whiteness onto the quarried limestone of Jerusalem, spilling over the straightness of its gap-toothed walls . . . over the unevenness of the structures within them . . . over the narrowness of its streets that connected the urban sprawl of shops and homes, along with the secular encroachments of Roman occupation.

In other places, shadowy places, Jesus' disciples hid in clumps of twos and threes. Tired. Despondent. Afraid.

In another part of the city, another disciple, Peter, sat by himself, slumped against an outcropping of rock, his arms wrapped around his knees, hugging them to keep himself from shaking. He had denied his king around a campfire where a peasant woman pointed him out as one of Jesus' followers. Three times Peter denied him. And when he did, he fled the heat from their stares and ran away weeping.

In still another part of the city, several of those who loved Jesus and watched him die were holed up in the second-story room where he ate his last supper. Patches of moonlight matted the floor, placed there by windows arching in the stone wall. In the shadows of that room, they cowered, lost among the shards of the shattered dream of a majestic king that was now gone and a magical kingdom that was not coming.

◆ ◆ ◆

In C. S. Lewis's classic Chronicles of Narnia, the true king of Narnia, a lion named Aslan, has been living in exile since the White Witch seized it, making it "always winter and never Christmas."

In this cold and brittle land, the witch ruled with a ruthless hand. Her spies were everywhere, watching for any threat to her rule, and, once reported, the threat was quickly and decisively dealt with.

Some were killed, others exiled, still others were turned into stone to decorate the courtyard of her expansive, turreted house. This is the courtyard that Lucy and Susan enter, where they see this menagerie of statues, frozen in place, as Aslan brings them to life.

"Oh, Susan! Look! Look at the lion!" Lucy exclaimed as she saw Aslan breathe on a smaller stone lion. And here is

Lewis's description of what happened next.

> I expect you've seen someone put a lighted match to a bit of newspaper which is propped up in a grate against an unlit fire. And for a second nothing seems to have happened; and then you notice a tiny streak of flame creeping along the edge of the newspaper. It was like that now. For a second after Aslan had breathed upon him the stone lion looked the same. Then a tiny streak of gold began to run along his white marble back—then it spread—then the color seemed to lick all over him as the flame licks over a bit of paper—then, while his hindquarters were still obviously stone, the lion shook his mane and all the heavy, stone folds rippled into living hair. Then he opened a great red mouth, warm and living, and gave a prodigious yawn. And now his legs had come to life. He lifted one of them and scratched himself. Then, having caught sight of Aslan, he went bounding after him and frisking round him, whimpering with delight and jumping up to lick his face.

The magic of Narnia is, of course, the miracle of the resurrection. At the darkest and most hopeless moment in the story, something more miraculous than make-believe happened. God breathed on the white statue in that cool, dark tomb. Life spread through it like a tiny streak of flame creeping along the edge of a newspaper. And Jesus stepped out of death into the fullness of life. The disciple who was closest to him described that first Easter:

> Early on the first day of the week, while it was still dark,

Mary Magdalene went to the tomb and saw that the stone had been removed from the entrance. So she came running to Simon Peter and the other disciple, the one Jesus loved, and said, "They have taken the Lord out of the tomb, and we don't know where they have put him!"

So Peter and the other disciple started for the tomb. Both were running, but the other disciple outran Peter and reached the tomb first. He bent over and looked in at the strips of linen lying there but did not go in. Then Simon Peter came along behind him and went straight into the tomb. He saw the strips of linen lying there, as well as the cloth that had been wrapped around Jesus' head. The cloth was still lying in its place, separate from the linen. Finally the other disciple, who had reached the tomb first, also went inside. He saw and believed. (They still did not understand from Scripture that Jesus had to rise from the dead.) Then the disciples went back to where they were staying.

Now Mary stood outside the tomb crying. As she wept, she bent over to look into the tomb and saw two angels in white, seated where Jesus' body had been, one at the head and the other at the foot.

They asked her, "Woman, why are you crying?"

"They have taken my Lord away," she said, "and I don't know where they have put him." At this, she turned around and saw Jesus standing there, but she did not realize that it was Jesus.

He asked her, "Woman, why are you crying? Who is it you are looking for?"

Thinking he was the gardener, she said, "Sir, if you have carried him away, tell me where you have put him, and I will get him."

Jesus said to her, "Mary."

She turned toward him and cried out in Aramaic, "Rabboni!" (which means "Teacher").

Jesus said, "Do not hold on to me, for I have not yet ascended to the Father. Go instead to my brothers and tell them, 'I am ascending to my Father and your Father, to my God and your God.'"

Mary Magdalene went to the disciples with the news: "I have seen the Lord!" And she told them that he had said these things to her.

On the evening of that first day of the week, when the disciples were together, with the doors locked for fear of the Jewish leaders, Jesus came and stood among them and said, "Peace be with you!" After he said this, he showed them his hands and side. The disciples were overjoyed when they saw the Lord.

Again Jesus said, "Peace be with you! As the Father has sent me, I am sending you." And with that he breathed on them and said, "Receive the Holy Spirit." (John 20:1-22)

With the warmth of his breath, Jesus breathed on his disciples the same breath that the Father had breathed onto him. A tiny streak of gold began to run along the white marble that their lives had become. And when the Spirit was poured forth on them in all its fullness, those followers of Christ bounded after him like the lion in Lewis's tale bounded after Aslan, frisking round him, so to speak, whimpering with delight and jumping up to lick his face.

No longer did they cower in the shadows. Now they stood in the public square. Luke tells the story in Acts 2:1-47:

> When the day of Pentecost came, they were all together in one place. Suddenly a sound like the blowing of a violent wind came from heaven and filled the whole house where they were sitting. They saw what seemed to be tongues of fire that separated and came to rest on each of them. All of them were filled with the Holy Spirit and began to speak in other tongues as the Spirit enabled them.
>
> Now there were staying in Jerusalem God-fearing Jews from every nation under heaven. When they heard this sound, a crowd came together in bewilderment, because each one heard their own language being spoken. Utterly amazed, they asked: "Aren't all these who are speaking Galileans? Then how is it that each of us hears them in our native language? Parthians, Medes and Elamites; residents of Mesopotamia, Judea and Cappadocia, Pontus and Asia, Phrygia and Pamphylia, Egypt and the parts of Libya near Cyrene; visitors from Rome (both Jews and converts to Judaism); Cretans and Arabs—we hear them declaring the wonders of God in our own tongues!" Amazed and perplexed, they asked one another, "What does this mean?"
>
> Some, however, made fun of them and said, "They have had too much wine."
>
> Then Peter stood up with the Eleven, raised his voice and addressed the crowd: "Fellow Jews and all of you who live in Jerusalem, let me explain this to you; listen

carefully to what I say. These people are not drunk, as you suppose. It's only nine in the morning! No, this is what was spoken by the prophet Joel:

"'In the last days, God says,
    I will pour out my Spirit on all people.
Your sons and daughters will prophesy,
    your young men will see visions,
    your old men will dream dreams
Even on my servants, both men and women,
    I will pour out my Spirit in those days,
    and they will prophesy.
I will show wonders in the heavens above
    and signs on the earth below,
    blood and fire and billows of smoke.
The sun will be turned to darkness
    and the moon to blood
    before the coming of the great and glorious day of
      the Lord.
And everyone who calls
    on the name of the Lord will be saved.'

"Fellow Israelites, listen to this: Jesus of Nazareth was a man accredited by God to you by miracles, wonders and signs, which God did among you through him, as you yourselves know. This man was handed over to you by God's deliberate plan and foreknowledge; and you, with the help of wicked men, put him to death by nailing him to the cross. But God raised him from the dead, freeing him from the agony of death, because it was impossible for death to keep its hold on him. David said about him:

"'I saw the Lord always before me.
    Because he is at my right hand,
    I will not be shaken.
Therefore my heart is glad and my tongue rejoices;
    my body also will rest in hope,
because you will not abandon me to the realm of the
        dead,
    you will not let your holy one see decay.
You have made known to me the paths of life;
    you will fill me with joy in your presence.'

"Fellow Israelites, I can tell you confidently that the patriarch David died and was buried, and his tomb is here to this day. But he was a prophet and knew that God had promised him on oath that he would place one of his descendants on his throne. Seeing what was to come, he spoke of the resurrection of the Messiah, that he was not abandoned to the realm of the dead, nor did his body see decay. God has raised this Jesus to life, and we are all witnesses of it. Exalted to the right hand of God, he has received from the Father the promised Holy Spirit and has poured out what you now see and hear. For David did not ascend to heaven, and yet he said,

"'The Lord said to my Lord:
    "Sit at my right hand
until I make your enemies
    a footstool for your feet."'

"Therefore let all Israel be assured of this: God has made this Jesus, whom you crucified, both Lord and Messiah."

When the people heard this, they were cut to the heart and said to Peter and the other apostles, "Brothers, what shall we do?"

Peter replied, "Repent and be baptized, every one of you, in the name of Jesus Christ for the forgiveness of your sins. And you will receive the gift of the Holy Spirit. The promise is for you and your children and for all who are far off—for all whom the Lord our God will call."

With many other words he warned them; and he pleaded with them, "Save yourselves from this corrupt generation." Those who accepted his message were baptized, and about three thousand were added to their number that day.

They devoted themselves to the apostles' teaching and to fellowship, to the breaking of bread and to prayer. Everyone was filled with awe at the many wonders and signs performed by the apostles. All the believers were together and had everything in common. They sold property and possessions to give to anyone who had need. Every day they continued to meet together in the temple courts. They broke bread in their homes and ate together with glad and sincere hearts, praising God and enjoying the favor of all the people. And the Lord added to their number daily those who were being saved.

Everywhere the statues were coming to life.
The courtyard no longer looked like a museum: it looked more like a zoo.

Frederick Buechner once said that the gospel is part tragedy, part comedy, part fairy tale. The tragedy is that we all in some way have Christ's blood on our hands. The comedy is that he loves us anyway and forgives us in all ways. The fairy tale is that there is a happily-ever-after ending not only to his story but to ours. And we, like him, will be transformed, in the twinkling of an eye, the way Cinderella was transformed on the way to the ball where her charming prince extended his hand and invited her to dance with him.

Until that great resurrection in the hereafter, we experience smaller resurrections in the here and now. One day our bodies will be renewed. Today it is our spirits.

As Jesus breathes on us, the cold stone within us comes to life.

Suddenly we see ourselves beautiful in the eyes of our beloved.

In a blushing moment that transcends any earthly joy we have experienced, he asks to take our hand . . .

And dance!

A PRAYER

Dear Father,

Thank you for the hope of the resurrection—
hope for all of us statues, longing to be free.
Thank you that this heavy, earthbound body of mine
will one day be released to flit about,
free from gravity, free from the downward pull of life.
free from death, free from decay,
free from sin, free from self.
Until that day, Lord,
grant that I could live a resurrected life,
here, now.
Help me to realize, as someone once said,
that nothing will be resurrected that has not first died.
Reveal that part of me, Lord,
the part that resists the cross, refuses the tomb.
Help me realize that resurrection is your work;
and that dying is mine.
In the precious name of Jesus,
who showed us not only how to live
but how to die.

Amen

FOR REFLECTION
AND CONVERSATION

"Everywhere the statues were coming to life." What are some ways God has brought you back to life? How did the experience change your relationship with him?

"Frederick Buechner once said that the gospel is part tragedy, part comedy, part fairy tale." Which of these descriptions of the gospel resonates with you the most? Why? What helps you to appreciate the other aspects of the gospel story?

In contrast to the author's discussion of sin, which "defaces" God's work in us, here the author assures us that by the intervention of the resurrected Christ, "suddenly we see ourselves beautiful in the eyes of our beloved." What accounts for the change?

Do you find it hard to "see yourself beautiful"? How can the meaning of the resurrection change your view of yourself?

Perhaps you've always found it easy to "see yourself beautiful." How does the resurrection change the way you see yourself?

What are some ways you can carry the good news of the resurrection to people in your life this week?

EPILOGUE

Michelangelo left behind some of the most magnificent sculptures the world has ever seen. *Madonna of the Stairs* was his earliest, which he finished when he was sixteen, followed by *Bacchus*, the *Pietà*, *David*, *Moses* and the tomb of Giuliano de' Medici, among others.

He attempted a total of forty-four.

He finished only fourteen.

Why he abandoned the others remains, for the most part, a mystery. Scholars have offered various theories. A demanding schedule that forced Michelangelo to travel to other cities to start other commissioned works. Defects in the marble. His disappointment in how the work was turning out.

Who knows for sure? The stones are silent.

Of the thirty sculptures the artist abandoned, here are three.

In 1506, Michelangelo began to sculpt a marble figure of St. Matthew, nearly nine feet high. It was to decorate the interior of Florence's Cathedral of Santa Maria del Fiore. The left knee and thigh of the sculpture are almost finished. The upper portion of the torso has been only superficially worked. The face is formed but only roughly.

Another unfinished work, begun in 1513, is called *The Dying Slave*. It was intended for the tomb of Julius II. The legs, torso and left arm are finished and polished. But the face is unhewn, as are the hands and feet.

Then there is the final work of his life, the Rondanini *Pietà*, on which he worked for ten years. Vasari writes that Michelangelo "ended up breaking the block, probably because the latter was full of impurities and so hard that sparks flew from under his chisel." The sculpture was rescued by a servant and survives to this day. It bears the marks of Michelangelo's chisel, but none of the beauty of his earlier *Pietà*.

If these stones could cry out, what would they say, I wonder?

And what, if anything, would they say to you and to me?

Sculptor Lorenzo Dominguez once summarized the dilemma of his work like this: "The stone wants to be stone; the artist wants it to be art."

The same dilemma exists for those of us who are the work of God's hands. In an attempt to free the image of Christ that is encased within the stone of the self, God begins chipping away everything that isn't Jesus. The stone either submits to the chipping or it resists.

If it submits, features of the Savior begin to emerge from our life. If it submits long enough, the Savior himself emerges. If, however, it resists, and continues to resist, there will come a day when God will let the stone be stone.

C. S. Lewis said as much when he stated that there are only two kinds of people in the end: those who say to God, "Thy will be done," and those to whom God says, "Okay, go ahead and have it your way."

Go ahead and have it your way.

You can imagine the restive stone, hearing those words and sighing in relief as the chiseling stops. As the torturer leaves, the stone rejoices. It is free! Free from the scrutiny of those eyes. Free from the tyranny of those tools. Free to be itself. Finally.

You can imagine the same stone, shrinking in shame when the artist's work is one day displayed. Who knew that all the endless chipping was leading to this one moment of unveiling? Its eyes downcast, the stone sees the chippage of its old self on the floor. It seems so inconsequential now, lying there, crushed underfoot, a gritty reminder of what it once was, of all it tried so tenaciously to hold on to.

There *will* be a time of unveiling, Paul says, not figuratively but in fact. This is how he describes it:

> I consider that our present sufferings are not worth comparing with the glory that will be revealed in us. For the creation waits in eager expectation for the children of God to be revealed. For the creation was subjected to frustration, not by its own choice, but by the will of the one who subjected it, in hope that the creation itself will be liberated from its bondage to decay and brought into the freedom and glory of the children of God. (Romans 8:18-21)

There will be a time when the groaning of creation will give way to a sigh of relief. At that time, we will share his glory.

"The promise of glory," wrote Lewis,

> is the promise, almost incredible and only possible by the work of Christ, that some of us, that any of us who really chooses, shall actually survive that examination, shall find approval, shall please God. To please God . . .

SHAPED BY THE CROSS

to be a real ingredient in the divine happiness . . . to be loved by God, not merely pitied, but delighted in as an artist delights in his work or a father in a son—it seems impossible, a weight or burden of glory which our thoughts can hardly sustain. But so it is.

God's delight in us will only be the beginning of our joy. Joy is not merely the absence of agony but the presence of ecstasy. Our joy will not only be the absence of slavery to sin and corruption, but the presence of a boundless freedom and the fragrant renewal of all creation. Our joy will not only be the absence of our most bitter enemy, but the presence of our most beloved friend. It will not simply be the absence of darkness, but the presence of God's glory that will magically illumine everything around us. It will not only be the absence of the thorns and nettles of nature's resistance, but the presence of Paradise, with the river of life shimmering through it and the tree of life growing out of it, with luscious and life-giving fruit hanging heavy on its branches. It will not only be the absence of death and sorrow and tears, but the presence of music and dancing and feasting at the wedding celebration of Christ and his church.

It was this joy, set before him, that gave Jesus the strength to endure his cross (Hebrews 12:2).

And it is what will give us the strength to endure ours.
Until that time, suffering has a voice in our life.
But though it has a voice, it does not have the last
    word.
The last word belongs to God.
And that word is *joy!*

At that word, the angel inside the marble will finally
    be set free.
All the angels will be set free.
The one we have loved for so long only from afar, we
    will then see face to face.
The beauty that is his will be ours.
So will the joy that is his.
So will the joy!